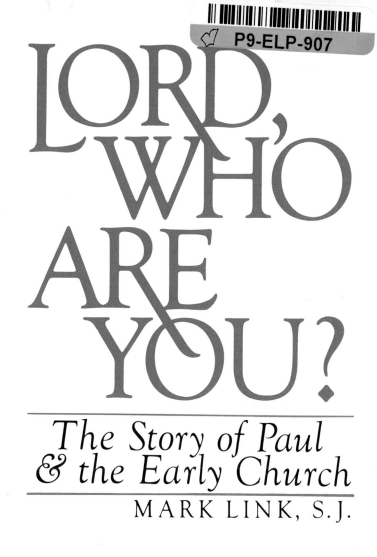

LORD, WHO ARE YOU?

The Story of Paul
& the Early Church

MARK LINK, S.J.

Argus Communications
A Division of **DLM,** Inc.
Allen, Texas 75002 U.S.A.

ACKNOWLEDGMENTS

Scripture quotations in this publication are from the *Good News Bible*—New Testament: Copyright © American Bible Society 1966, 1971, 1976. Used by permission.

Excerpts from *The Acts of the Apostles* (Revised Edition), translated with an Introduction and Interpretation by William Barclay. Copyright © 1976 William Barclay. Used by permission of The Westminster Press and The Saint Andrew Press, Edinburgh.

Excerpts from *Ambassador for Christ* by William Barclay. Copyright © 1974 Judson Press. Used by permission of Judson Press.

Excerpts from "Night Voices" by Dietrich Bonhoeffer, trans. by Keith R. Crim in *I Loved This People*. Copyright © M. E. Bratcher 1965. Used by permission of John Knox Press.

Excerpts from *The Interpreter's Bible*, Vol. IX, *The Acts, Romans*, ed. by George A. Buttrick. Copyright 1954. Used by permission of Abingdon Press.

Excerpt from *Letters from the Desert* by Carlo Carretto, trans. by Rose Mary Hancock. Published and © 1972 by Orbis Books and Darton Longman & Todd Ltd. Reprinted by permission of Orbis Books and Darton Longman & Todd Ltd.

Excerpt from *This Hallowed Ground: The Story of the Union Side of the Civil War* by Bruce Catton. Copyright © 1955, 1956 by Bruce Catton. Reprinted by permission of Doubleday & Co., Inc.

Continued on page 213

Cover Photo

In the shadow of the acropolis, which is crowned by the Parthenon, Paul gave his famous speech to the "men of Athens" (Acts 17:22-31).

Book design by Lydia Halverson
Maps by Betty Raskins

Copyright © 1982 Mark Link

Printed in the United States of America

Argus Communications
A Division of DLM, Inc.
One DLM Park
Allen, Texas 75002 U.S.A.

International Standard Book Number: 0-89505-066-8

Library of Congress Catalog Card Number: 82-70106

0 9 8 7 6 5 4 3 2 1

CONTENTS

PREFACE

It was finished! All over! Ended!

But three days later
an incredible event took place.
The crushed followers of Jesus
were amazingly transformed.
"Jesus is risen!"

What happened next
is described in Acts, Letters, and Revelation.
The Christian community emerges,
reaches out, and embraces the world.
It retraces the footsteps of Jesus—
preaching, healing, loving, praying, suffering.

The driving force of the community is the Holy Spirit.
And one of the persons
most sensitive to the Spirit's prompting
is an unexpected newcomer named Paul.
It is Paul's calling
that inspired the title for this book.

Suddenly
a light from the sky flashed around him.
He fell to the ground
and heard a voice saying to him,
"Saul, Saul! Why do you persecute me?"

"Who are you, Lord?" he asked.

"I am Jesus, whom you persecute,"
the voice said.

ACTS 9:3–5

It is hoped
that this book will be a "road to Damascus"
along which other travelers
will make Paul's question their own.

For those who teach this book
in a school or study-group setting,
two helpful aids are available:
a *Teacher Manual*
and a *Blackline Master Kit* of "handouts"
relating each chapter to daily life.

Easter, 1982   Mark Link, S.J.

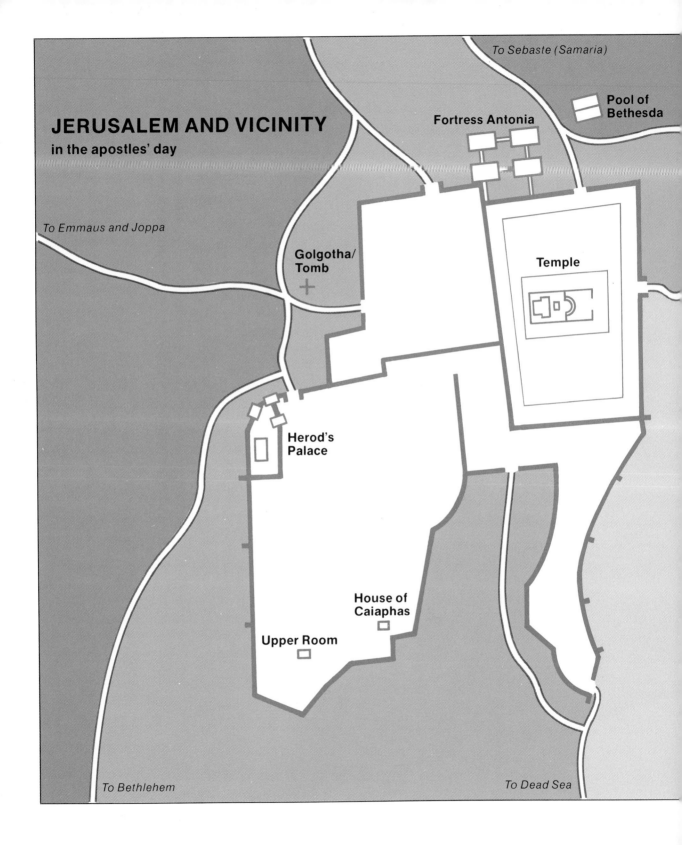

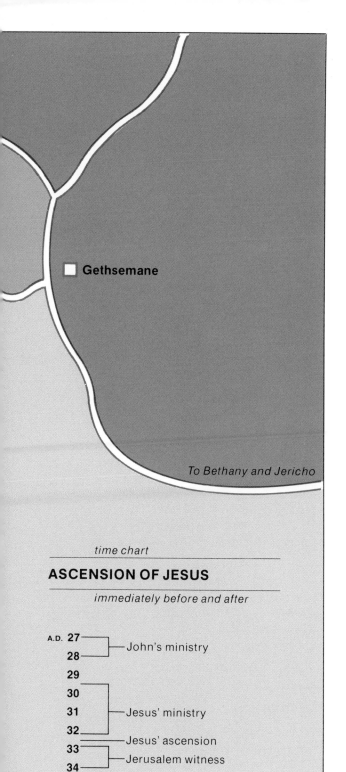

Gethsemane

To Bethany and Jericho

time chart

ASCENSION OF JESUS

immediately before and after

A.D. 27 — ┐
           ├— John's ministry
     28 — ┘

     29

     30 — ┐
     31 — ├— Jesus' ministry
     32 — ┘
        ── Jesus' ascension
     33 — ┐
        ── Jerusalem witness
     34 — ┘

JERUSALEM

Acts 1-7

1

The Storm's Eye

A giant television tower
soars above the skyline of East Berlin.
Slightly below the tip of the tower
is a revolving restaurant.
East German officials intended the edifice
to be a Communist showpiece to the West.
But a fluke in design
turned it into an unexpected embarrassment.

"The Cross Over East Germany"
R. D. LINDER AND R. V. PIERARD

Whenever the sun
shines on the spherical rotating restaurant
atop the modernistic structure,
a glittering cross appears.
East German officials
even ordered the exterior painted over
in a recent attempt to blot out the cross,
but to no avail.

UNEXPECTED

Something similar happened in Jerusalem
after Jesus' crucifixion.
Officials hoped the death of Jesus
would blot out the movement he began.
Instead of blotting it out, however,
it set in motion a chain of events
that had just the opposite effect.

The movement spread so spectacularly
that by A.D. 64
the Roman emperor, Nero, made Christians
the target of an all-out persecution.

How did Christianity, in 30 short years,
grow from a tiny mustard seed
into such a spectacular, towering tree?
This amazing story
unfolds in the Acts of the Apostles.

BOOK OF FEATS

The word *Acts* was used by ancient writers
to refer to the feats of great leaders.
Thus we have the Acts of Hercules,
the Acts of Hannibal, the Acts of Alexander.

The Acts of the Apostles
models itself after such writings.
But Acts is not a complete record
of the feats of all of the apostles.
It is only a partial record
of some of them—notably Peter and Paul.

The first remarkable thing about Acts
is its introduction. It reads:

Dear Theophilus:

In my first book I wrote about
all the things that Jesus did and taught
from the time he began his work
until the day he was taken up to heaven.

ACTS 1:1-2

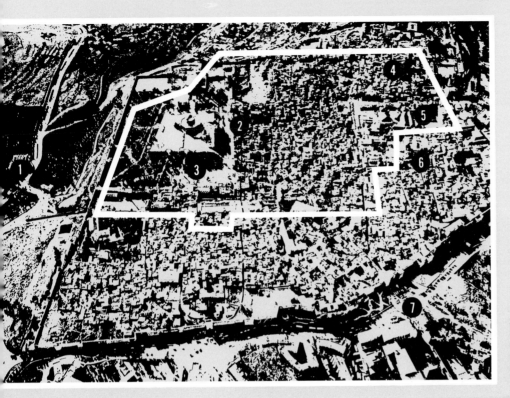

1 Mount of Olives,
2 Western Wall,
3 Temple Area,
4 Last Supper Room,
5 Herod's Palace,
6 Golgotha/Tomb,
7 Modern Damascus Gate

What Would You See?

If you stepped into a "time machine"
and traveled backward into history
to Jesus' Jerusalem, how would the city look?
One answer to that question may be found
by looking closely at this aerial view
of Jerusalem's Old City as it appears today.

The white-line overlay
shows the probable location of the city walls
in Jesus' day.

The temple area identifies the exact spot
where the temple stood in Jesus' time.
(A Muslim shrine, the Dome of the Rock,
has occupied the spot since about A. D. 700.)

Some scholars suggest the apostles gathered
to await the Spirit (Acts 1:13)
in the very room where the Last Supper
was celebrated—a room belonging to
the mother of Mark (Acts 12:12).

This introduction parallels the introduction
to the Gospel according to Luke:

Dear Theophilus:

*Many people have done their best
to write a report of the things*
*that have taken place among us. . . .
And so, Your Excellency,
because I have carefully studied
all these matters from their beginning,
I thought it would be good
to write an orderly account for you.*

LUKE 1:1-3

It is clear that Luke intended Acts
to continue his Gospel
and tell the story of Christianity's growth
during the 30 years after Jesus' crucifixion.

Luke the Historian in Recent Study
C. K. BARRETT

*And so, the events narrated in Acts
point to a new thrust that begins to take place
in the early Christian community.
It ceases to be a church "waiting for the end"
and becomes a dynamic, out-going church,
"working for the end."*

The "seed" of the kingdom planted by Jesus
is now watered and cultivated by his followers.

The driving force and inspiration
behind the early Christian community
was the Holy Spirit.
And it is to the Holy Spirit
that the attention of Acts immediately turns.

ASCENSION OF JESUS

*For forty days after his death
[Jesus] appeared to [his disciples] many times
in ways that proved beyond doubt
that he was alive. . . .*

*He gave them this order:
"Do not leave Jerusalem,
but wait for the gift I told you about,
the gift my Father promised.
John baptized with water,
but in a few days you will be baptized
with the Holy Spirit.". . .*

*"When the Holy Spirit comes upon you,
you will be filled with power,
and you will be witnesses for me*

*in Jerusalem, in all of Judea and Samaria,
and to the ends of the earth."
After saying this,
he was taken up to heaven
as they watched him,
and a cloud hid him from their sight.*

*They still had their eyes
fixed on the sky as he went away,
when two men dressed in white
suddenly stood beside them and said,
"Galileans, why are you standing there
looking up at the sky?
This Jesus, who was taken from you
into heaven, will come back in the same way
that you saw him go to heaven."*

ACTS 1:3-11

As suddenly as the "two men" appeared,
they vanished, leaving the apostles filled
with questions.

The two men said Jesus would come back,
but they did not say when.
At this point, his disciples assumed
that this would be in their own lifetime.

They might have compared this time
to the "eye" of a hurricane,
that electrifying, breathtaking lull
between the first half of the storm
and its trailing second half.

Or to use another image,
they viewed this time as the pregnant pause
between "the lightning of Jesus' first coming"
and "the thunder of his second coming."

As the disciples left the Mount of Olives
and retraced their steps to Jerusalem,
two of Jesus' statements drummed in their ears.

First, don't leave Jerusalem
until the "Holy Spirit comes upon you."

OΛΓΟC·ΠΑΥΛΟC

"Luke, our dear doctor,
and Demas send you their greetings."
Colossians 4:14

Who Was Luke?

Luke is cited three times
in Paul's letters: Colossians 4:14,
2 Timothy 4:11, Philemon 24.

Two facts emerge from these references:
Luke was a doctor,
and Luke occasionally traveled with Paul.
A third fact—that Luke was a Gentile—
may be inferred from Colossians 4:11-14.

A question arises.
Where did Luke get his information for Acts?
Here we must distinguish between
the first half of Acts and the second half.

The first half deals mainly
with three Christian communities:
Jerusalem, Caesarea, and Antioch.
Luke probably got much of this information
from Christians living in these communities.

The second half deals mainly
with Paul's journeys and preaching.
Luke possibly got much of his information
from traveling and talking with Paul.
The "we" sections in Acts
(16:10-17, 20:5-16, 21:1-18, 27:1-28:16)
have been cited as possible evidence of this.

11

Second, "when the Holy Spirit comes upon you,
you will be filled with power,
and you will be witnesses for me
in Jerusalem, in all of Judea and Samaria,
and to the ends of the earth."

This second statement provided the outline
for Luke's presentation in Acts:

1   witness in Jerusalem (chapters 1-7),
2   witness in Judea and Samaria (8-12),
3   witness to the world (13-28).

DAYS OF SUSPENSE

In the days that followed,
the disciples prepared for the Spirit's coming.

They gathered frequently
to pray as a group, together with the women
and with Mary the mother of Jesus
and with his brothers.

ACTS 1:14

Significantly, it is not just the 11 apostles
who gathered frequently to pray.
Luke notes that at one of the meetings
120 people were present (Acts 1:15).

What Are They Saying about Luke and Acts?
ROBERT J. KARRAS

The number 120 is suggestive
of the formation of a new community,
for rabbinic law has it
that 120 inhabitants are necessary
for a town to have a small sanhedrin.

Significantly, also, Mary and the other women
were among those waiting
to be formed into a "witnessing community"
by the promised coming of the Spirit.

As they waited,
the group decided to choose someone
to replace the dead Judas.
The qualifications were simple. Peter says:

"He must be one of the men
who were in our group during the whole time
that the Lord Jesus traveled about with us,
beginning from the time
John preached his message of baptism
until the day
Jesus was taken up from us to heaven."

So they proposed two men: Joseph,
who was called Barsabbas
(also known as Justus), and Matthias.
Then they prayed,
"Lord, you know the thoughts of everyone,
so show us which of these two
you have chosen to serve as an apostle
in the place of Judas. . . ."
Then they drew lots to choose . . .
and the one chosen was Matthias.

ACTS 1:22-26

Choosing a replacement by drawing lots
may seem strange to us.
For Jews, however, it was normal.
This is how Joshua divided land (Joshua 18:6).
It is also how the Israelites
assigned certain jobs (Judges 20:6).

Drawing lots was a way
to keep human feelings and prejudices
from influencing important decisions.
But beyond this, it was a way
to put an outcome in God's hands.
If God had a preference about something,
drawing lots was a good way
to let him show it.
For biblical Jews, God's will
was more important than life itself.

2 Wind and Fire

A little boy
received a model sailboat for his birthday.
He was so excited he couldn't sit still.
He began running about the house,
showing it to everyone.

The One and Only Me
IRENE CHAMPERNOWNE

But that was not enough.
He could not contain himself.
So at last he went to the window
and looking up at the sky
he said desperately,
"Oh God! Have you seen my boat?"
There was a moment's pause and silence,
as if the child
were waiting for an answer from God.
Then suddenly he turned from the window
to his mother and asked,
"What is God like . . . ?"

His mother was taken aback
and did not know what answer to give
to such a deep question.

While she was pausing
to figure out what answer to give the boy,
he suddenly blurted out excitedly:
"I know! He's the wind!"

Ancient Jews would have applauded
the little boy's insight.
They, too, saw a parallel between the wind
and God.

WIND IMAGE

The unseen wind's breathlike touch
and galelike force spoke to the Jews
of God's own unseen presence and power.
The prophet Ezekiel says:

God said to me,
"Mortal man, prophesy to the wind . . .
to come from every direction,
to breathe into these dead bodies,
and to bring them back to life."

So I prophesied . . .
and they came to life and stood up.

EZEKIEL 37:9–10

The wind image was also used by Jesus
to speak of the Spirit's life-giving coming
in baptism. He says:

"The wind blows wherever it wishes."

JOHN 3:8

FIRE IMAGE

Fire is another Old Testament image
frequently associated with God's activity
in human affairs.

Thus God's first appearance to Moses
was set against a background of fire.
Seeing a bush afire, but not burning up,
Moses says:

13

Jews traveling to Jerusalem
for temple celebrations
sometimes had to traverse the "desert."
Our English word *desert*,
when used of the Bible,
can mean one of three different regions:
stretches of sand, like the above;
stretches of rock, with occasional springs;
semiarid stretches, with just enough growth
to support scrounging goats and sheep.

"Why isn't the bush burning up?
I will go closer and see."

When the Lord saw
that Moses was coming closer, he called
to him from the middle of the bush. . . .
So Moses covered his face,
because he was afraid to look at God.

EXODUS 3:3-6

Later, God's giving of the Law to Moses
took place against a background of fire.

There was thunder and lightning. . . .
All of Mount Sinai was covered with smoke,
because the Lord had come down on it in fire.

EXODUS 19:16-18

COMBINED IMAGE

Finally,
the coming of the messianic era was linked
to the combined image of wind and fire.

The Lord will come with fire.
He will ride on the wings of a storm.

ISAIAH 66:15

It is in light of this Old Testament imagery
that we must read and interpret
Luke's account of what occurred in Jerusalem
on the Jewish celebration of Pentecost.

NOISE AND UPROAR

Passover, Pentecost, and Tabernacles—
these were Israel's three big celebrations.
During each of these festive periods,
Jews within reasonable distance of Jerusalem
came to worship in the temple.
Jews living greater distances away
tried to come to Jerusalem for these feasts
at least once during a lifetime.

Here we must note that long before Jesus,
Jews had spread across the ancient world
as far as Rome itself.
This explains why, on Pentecost,
Jerusalem was packed with people
not only from Judea but also from other lands.

Pentecost itself
was a thanksgiving celebration,

combining gratitude for the year's harvest
with gratitude for the giving of the Law
to Moses on Mount Sinai.
It took its name
from the Greek word for "fiftieth"
because it occurred 50 days after Passover.
This meant it usually fell in June,
when travel conditions were best.
We read in Acts:

When the day of Pentecost came,
all the believers
were gathered together in one place.
Suddenly there was a noise from the sky
which sounded like a strong wind blowing,
and it filled the whole house
where they were sitting.
Then they saw what looked like
tongues of fire which spread out
and touched each person there.
They were all filled with the Holy Spirit
and began to talk in other languages,
as the Spirit enabled them to speak.

ACTS 2:1-4

The noise and uproar
attracted a huge crowd out in the street.
The amazed onlookers exclaimed:

"Some of us are from Rome,
both Jews and Gentiles converted to Judaism,
and some of us are from Crete and Arabia—
yet all of us hear them speaking
in our own languages
about the great things that God has done!"
Amazed and confused, they kept asking
each other, "What does this mean?"

But others made fun of the believers,
saying, "These people are drunk!"

ACTS 2:10-13

Two different gifts of tongues are implied
in Luke's dramatic description:
speaking ecstatically
and speaking in another language.

The first gift spawns the mocking slur:
"Those people are drunk!"
This gift of ecstatic prayer,
sometimes referred to as *glossolalia,*
was common in the early Christian community.
One purpose it served
was to act as a visible sign of confirmation.

What Are They Saying about Luke and Acts?
ROBERT J. KARRAS

Luke uses the phenomenon
of speaking in tongues as an external sign
of the Spirit's ratification of the Church's
move into a new missionary phase. . . .
Acts 8:14-18 occurs in the context
of the Gospel moving into the territory
of the Samaritans. . . .
Acts 10:44-46 occurs in the context
of the missionary expansion to pagans
in the person of Cornelius. . . .
Acts 19:6 concerns missionary activity
among a "fringe group,"
the disciples of John the Baptist.
Through glossolalia the Spirit gives notice
to all that he puts his stamp of approval
on these missionary endeavors.

The church's first missionary outreach
on Pentecost is stamped with visible approval.

The second gift of tongues recalls
the Tower of Babel episode (Genesis 11:9),
where a confusion of tongues is portrayed.
The Spirit's coming on Pentecost reverses Babel.
What sin split apart, the Spirit now unites.
The Pentecost event is intended not just for Jews
but for all nations.

FILLED WITH POWER

The greatest gift of Pentecost, however,
is the "gift of tongues,"
which empowered the apostles "to proclaim
God's message with boldness" (Acts 4:31).

It is this gift that empowered Jesus' followers
to proclaim the Good News courageously,
uncompromisingly, and enthusiastically,
even in the face of overwhelming opposition.
It is the power promised by Jesus.

*Peter stood up with the other eleven apostles
and in a loud voice
began to speak to the crowd:*

*"Fellow Jews . . . this is what
the prophet Joel spoke about . . .
'God says:
I will pour out my Spirit on everyone . . .
and they will proclaim my message.*

This island of paved stone (partially shown)
marks the area where the temple once stood.
A Muslim shrine, the Dome of the Rock
(not shown), marks the exact spot.
Beneath the dome lies a 40-by-60-foot rock,
said to be the site
where Abraham led Isaac to be sacrificed.
David chose this spot for the temple.

I will perform miracles in the sky above
and wonders on the earth below . . .
before the great
and glorious Day of the Lord comes.
And then, whoever calls out to the Lord
for help will be saved.'"

ACTS 2:14-21

Day of the Lord—
this phrase echoed in the ears of the crowd
like the blast of a trumpet.
Few ideas influenced Israel's history as it did.
The Day of the Lord
was that moment in the history of humankind
when God would intervene
to exalt his chosen people above the nations.

Just as Christians divide history
into before and after Christ,
Jews divided history
into before and after the Day of the Lord.

This is Peter's message:
What you see today are signs announcing
the beginning of the Day of the Lord.
The end of the Day of the Lord
will be Jesus' return (Acts 1:11).

The Acts of the Apostles
NEAL M. FLANAGAN

Joel saw the beginning and the end
of the messianic era alongside one another
without strict time sequence
and spoke of them as such.
Peter does the same.
The message is the important thing. . . .
Salvation is promised to him . . .
who confesses that Jesus is God. . . .
That Jesus is Christ (Messiah) and Lord,
Peter will now prove from Scripture.

FILLED WITH AWE

Peter continues:

"Listen to these words, fellow Israelites!
Jesus of Nazareth was a man whose
divine authority was clearly proven to you
by all the miracles and wonders
which God performed through him.
You yourselves know this,
for it happened here among you. . . .
You killed him by letting sinful men
crucify him.
But God raised him from death . . .
and we are all witnesses to this fact.
He has been raised to the right side
of God, his Father, and has received
from him the Holy Spirit, as he promised.
What you now see and hear is his gift
that he has poured out on us. . . .

"All the people of Israel, then,
are to know for sure that this Jesus,
whom you crucified, is the one
that God has made Lord and Messiah!"

When the people heard this,
they were deeply troubled
and said to Peter and the other apostles,
"What shall we do, brothers?"

Peter said to them,
"Each one of you
must turn away from his sins
and be baptized in the name of Jesus Christ,
so that your sins will be forgiven;
and you will receive
God's gift, the Holy Spirit. . . ."

Many of them believed his message
and were baptized,
and about three thousand people
were added to the group that day.

How Did He Do It?

No tape recorder was running
to record Peter's Pentecost speech.
No scribe was on hand to take notes.

This raises an important question:
How did Luke go about
composing the many speeches in Acts?
(Nearly a third of the book is given over to them.)

Luke undoubtedly reconstructed the speeches
from the material available to him.
Probably shorter than the original,
the reconstructed speeches were often
only a summary of what was probably said.

A fourth-century B.C. historian
wrote concerning the speeches he reported:

History of the Peloponnesian War
THUCYDIDES

*I have found it difficult
to retain a memory of the precise words
which I had heard spoken;
so it was with those who brought me reports.
But I have made the persons say
what it seemed to me most opportune
for them to say in view of each situation;
at the same time,
I have adhered as closely as possible to
the general sense of what was actually said.*

Luke undoubtedly
followed this same procedure in Acts.
In some cases, as in the "we" sections,
he may have worked from excellent notes
scribbled down in his "travel journal."

In other cases, as in early Acts,
Luke was not present for the speech
and had to rely on his own historical research,
the recollections of others,
or his own inspired theological insight
Concerning this latter point,
this observation has been made:

"Acts of the Apostles"
RICHARD J. DILLON AND JOSEPH A. FITZMYER

*Luke does not so much write
a "history" of the early Church,
or an early Christian apologetic,
as he does a theological essay that describes,
somewhat idyllically, the character, growth
and problems of the early Church for the sake
of Gentiles or Gentile-Christian readers.*

Concerning the "speeches" in Acts, specifically,
this observation has been made:

Dictionary of the Bible
JOHN L. MCKENZIE

*"Their historical value
lies in their faithful preservation
of the themes of the primitive preaching
rather than in their exact agreement
with the situation." (L. Cerfaux)*

This Mount Sinai view recalls Exodus 19:16–18:

"The people . . . stood at the foot of the mountain. . . .
The LORD had come down on it in fire."

The Upper Room was a new Mount Sinai, upon which
the Lord descended in fire to forge a new covenant
with his new people.

They spent their time
in learning from the apostles,
taking part in the fellowship,
and sharing in the fellowship meals
and the prayers.

Many miracles and wonders
were being done through the apostles,
and everyone was filled with awe.

ACTS 2:22–24, 32–43

The gift of the Holy Spirit on Pentecost
transformed the 120 followers of Jesus
into a "witnessing community"
that filled all who saw them "with awe."
The gift of the Holy Spirit transformed them,
also, into a "sharing community"
that met together
to study, to pray, and to "break bread."

Beggars still may be seen
in the streets of modern Jerusalem.

*We falter, ashamed of our strong step,
and noticing this she gazes up
clear-eyed, without resentment—
it seems much worse that she is pretty.
In Bengal, GS says stiffly,
beggars will break their children's knees
to achieve this pitiable effect
for business purposes:
this is his way of expressing his distress. . . .
I long to give her something—a new life?—
yet am afraid to tamper with such dignity.
And so I smile as best I can, and say
"Namas-te!" "Good morning!" How absurd!*

The comment about Bengal beggars
recalls the words of Euripides, the dramatist:

*Poverty possesses this sickness:
it teaches people to do what is evil.*

ANCIENT BEGGARS

Jesus told a parable
of a servant about to be fired.

*"The servant said to himself,
'My master is going to dismiss me. . . .
What shall I do?
I am not strong enough to dig ditches,
and I am ashamed to beg.'"*

LUKE 16:3

The servant's words
reflect the ancient attitude toward begging.
It is put vividly in Sirach 40:28-29:

*Son, don't live the life of a beggar;
it is better to die than to beg.
If you have to depend on someone else
for your food,
you are not really living your own life.*

3
Rise and Walk!

A modern adventurer
describes this sight as he and a companion
start a 250-mile hike across the Himalayas.

The Snow Leopard
PETER MATTHIESSEN

*We take breakfast in the village tea house,
and are under way well before seven.*

*A child dragging bent useless legs
is crawling up the hill outside the village.
Nose to the stones . . .
she pulls herself along like a broken cricket.*

Yet, in New Testament times,
economic conditions got so bad in Judea
that more than a few people had to beg.
If you happened to be blind or crippled,
you had no choice.

Ancient beggars
often sat outside places of worship.
Their thinking was that people
on their way to pray
were more disposed to give another help.
Thus beggars used to congregate
at the temple gates in Jerusalem,
especially at the three times of daily prayer:
nine in the morning, noon,
and three in the afternoon.

How important these hours of prayer were
is clear from the Book of Daniel.
When the young prophet was in exile,
he kept these hours of prayer,
even at great personal risk.

In an upstairs room of his house
there were windows
that faced toward Jerusalem.
There, just as he had always done,
he knelt down at the open windows
and prayed to God three times a day.

When Daniel's enemies
observed him praying to God,
all of them went together to the king
to accuse Daniel. They said,
"Your Majesty . . .
Daniel, one of the exiles from Judah,
does not respect Your Majesty
or obey the order you issued.
He prays regularly three times a day."

DANIEL 6:10-13

It is against this background
that we should read chapter 3 in Acts.

One day Peter and John went to the Temple
at three o'clock in the afternoon,
the hour for prayer.
There at the Beautiful Gate, as it was called,
was a man who had been lame all his life.
Every day he was carried to the gate
to beg for money from the people
who were going into the Temple.
When he saw Peter and John going in,
he begged them to give him something.
They looked straight at him, and Peter said,
"Look at us!"
So he looked at them,
expecting to get something from them.
But Peter said to him,
"I have no money at all,
but I give you what I have:
in the name of Jesus Christ of Nazareth
I order you to get up and walk!"
Then he took him by his right hand
and helped him up.
At once the man's feet and ankles
became strong; he jumped up, stood on
his feet, and started walking around.
Then he went into the Temple with them,
walking and jumping and praising God.
The people there saw him walking
and praising God,
and when they recognized him as the beggar
who had sat at the Beautiful Gate,
they were all surprised and amazed
at what had happened to him.

ACTS 3:1-10

GIFT FROM GOD

Few biblical scenes have been so humanly
and beautifully portrayed as this one.
The lame beggar looks at Peter and John.
He extends his arm and cups his hand,
"expecting to get something from them."
A long minute of silence goes by.

The Explosion

The Interpreter's Bible
GEORGE A. BUTTRICK, EDITOR

The atomic bomb is a fact.
It is not a physicist's hope;
it is not a chemist's dream.
It went off at 8:15 A.M. Japanese time,
August 6, 1945. It is something done.
That is where we begin with Jesus.
The birth, life, and death of Jesus
are facts of recorded history.
The whole reality of that career . . .
is not a pious hope or a dream.
It is something that happened. . . .
It can be dated; it can be timed.

Something else is true, also.
The people
whose lives were changed most by the atomic bomb
are the ones who saw it explode at Hiroshima,
or the ones who have met Japanese
who were at Hiroshima on August 6, 1945.

It is the same with Jesus.
You can read about him, think about him,
dream about him.
But you will never fully understand him
until the risen Jesus explodes in your heart.
When this explosion takes place,
Jesus stops being a name on a page
and becomes a person very much alive
and at the center of your life.

Then Peter places in the beggar's hand,
not a coin, but a new life from God.

Like so many pray-ers,
the beggar ends up thanking God
for refusing him what he fervently prayed for
and giving him something far greater.
Elizabeth Barrett Browning wrote:

God's gifts put man's best dreams to shame.

SIGN FROM GOD

Luke's portrayal of the beggar's reaction
to his unexpected cure
is even more human and beautiful
than the scene that preceded it.

First, the beggar clasps Peter's hand.
Then, he is pulled shakily to his feet.
Next, he takes a few wobbly steps.
Finally, he runs and prances up and down
like an excited child—praising God.
He cannot contain himself.
No longer is he condemned to sit and beg.

In his unrestrained joy and excitement,
the beggar becomes an eloquent witness
to the "signs" Isaiah said would trumpet
the arrival of the age of the Messiah.

Tell everyone . . .
the blind will be able to see,
and the deaf will hear.
The lame will leap and dance,
and those who cannot speak
will shout for joy.

ISAIAH 35:4-6

This is the same prophecy Jesus cited
to assure the disciples of John the Baptist
that the age of the Messiah had arrived
(Luke 7:21-23).

What Happened to It?

Jesus loved the temple.
He called it his "Father's house" (John 2:16).
He taught in it daily (Matthew 26:55).
But at the moment of Jesus' death,
something happened:
"The curtain hanging in the Temple
was torn in two" (Matthew 27:51).

From that moment on,
the temple declined rapidly in Jewish history.
True to Jesus' prophecy (Matthew 24:1-2),
it was totally destroyed in A.D. 70.

Where is the temple now?
Paul explains.
Writing to Christians at Corinth, he says:
"Surely you know
that you are God's temple" (1 Corinthians 3:16).

1 Temple, **2** Court of Priests, **3** Court of Israel (Men), **4** Beautiful Gate (Acts 3:2), **5** Court of Women, **6** Gentile Barrier (Acts 21:28), **7** Solomon's Porch (Acts 3:11)

23

The power that was in Jesus
was now present and active in his apostles.
They inherited
the mission and the authority of Jesus.
Even those who opposed the apostles
could not deny what was happening.

"What shall we do with these men? . . .
Everyone in Jerusalem knows
that this extraordinary miracle
has been performed by them,
and we cannot deny it."

ACTS 4:16

REPENT

Peter spoke to the people about the miracle:

"Fellow Israelites,
why are you surprised at this . . . ?
Do you think
that it was by means of our own power
or godliness that we made this man walk?
The God of Abraham, Isaac, and Jacob,
the God of our ancestors,
has given divine glory to his Servant Jesus. . . .
You rejected him in Pilate's presence. . . .
You killed the one who leads to life,
but God raised him from death. . . .
It was the power of his name
that gave strength to this lame man. . . .

"God announced long ago through all
the prophets that his Messiah had to suffer;
and he made it come true in this way.
Repent, then, and turn to God,
so that he will forgive your sins.
If you do, times of spiritual strength
will come from the Lord,
and he will send Jesus, who is the Messiah
he has already chosen for you.
He must remain in heaven until
the time comes for all things to be made new,

as God announced
through his holy prophets of long ago. . . .
The promises of God . . .
are for you, and you share in the covenant
which God made with your ancestors.
As he said to Abraham,
'Through your descendants
I will bless all the people on earth.'"

ACTS 3:12-25

Like Peter's discourse on Pentecost,
Luke portrays this one as taking place
in an unscheduled and unplanned way.
It was triggered by the crowd's reaction
to the cure of the blind beggar.

Peter's words, as Luke presents them,
reflect the early church's conviction
about Jesus.

FIVE FACTS

Scholars sometimes group Christian preaching
into four kinds:

kerygma, proclaiming the word;
didache, explaining the word;
periklesis, exhorting people to live the word;
homilia, applying the word to daily life.

The kind of preaching found in Acts
is mainly kerygma, proclaiming the Good News.
Over and over,
five facts are stressed about Jesus:

1   he suffered, died, rose (3:15),
2   he fulfilled the prophecies (3:18, 21ff),
3   he is the Messiah (3:18, 20),
4   he calls to repentance (3:19),
5   he will come again (3:21).

4
Storm Clouds

Mark Twain said:

Most people
are bothered by those passages in Scripture
which they cannot understand;
but as for me,
I always noticed that the passages in Scripture
which trouble me most
are those which I do understand.

A Scripture passage that we all understand
and that troubles many people
is Jesus' words about suffering for the Gospel.

"You will be arrested and taken to court. . . .
You will stand before rulers and kings
for my sake to tell them the Good News. . . .
And when you are arrested
and taken to court, do not worry . . .
about what you are going to say;
when the time comes,
say whatever is then given to you.
For the words you speak will not be yours;
they will come from the Holy Spirit."

MARK 13:9-11

When Peter and John heard Jesus say this
at sunset one evening a few months before,
they had no idea
how quickly these events would take place.
Now it happened.

Thus Luke returns again
to a prominent theological theme in Acts:
the life and experience of the early church
paralleled in a striking way
the life and experience of Jesus.
As Jesus suffered for his own prophetic witness,
so did his disciples.

ACTION

The cure of the lame beggar
was like letting a tiger loose in a village.
News traveled fast
inside the walls of Jerusalem.
Within minutes everyone was talking about it.
And within minutes
the great shadow of religious authority
hung over the heads of Peter and John
like a giant storm cloud.

The episode created a big stir
not only because of the healing involved
but also because of the new dimension
it suddenly introduced into the preaching
of the apostles—that of concrete action.

The importance of this dimension
has been put many ways by many people.
Edgar Guest, a poet, said:
"I'd rather see a sermon than hear one any day."
Robert Frost put it this way
in "A Masque of Reason":
"Society can never think things out:
It has to see them acted out by actors."

When the dimension of action is added to talk,
that's when things really start to happen.

25

*But so long as an idea is only talked about
it does little harm. . . .
In the middle of the nineteenth century
no one minded when men talked against slavery,
but when those same men took steps
to set the slaves free, they found opposition
that was not easily overcome.*

ARREST

And so it happened
that when Peter and John cured the beggar,
they opened the door to trouble.

*Peter and John
were still speaking to the people
when some priests,
the officer in charge of the temple guards,
and some Sadducees arrived.*

ACTS 4:1

At first, the authorities stood in the back
and did nothing but listen.
Within a short time, however,
they revised their original strategy.

*They were annoyed
because the two apostles were teaching
the people that Jesus had risen from death,
which proved that the dead will rise to life.*

ACTS 4:2

This kind of talk offended the Sadducees
who denied an afterlife.
On more than one occasion
they had challenged Jesus on this point
(Matthew 22:23-32).
Using their influence with the officer and
the guards, the Sadducees made their move
against Peter and John.

*They arrested them and put them in jail
until the next day, since it was already late.*

ACTS 4:3

This arrest began another new dimension
in the life of Jesus' first followers.
For the first time,
they experienced the persecution
foretold by Jesus and experienced by him.
The life of the young church began,
more and more, to resemble and parallel
the life of Jesus.

TRIAL

The next day Peter and John
were asked to give an account of their actions
before the Jewish Council, the Sanhedrin.
This body of 71 members included priests,
scribes, and elders of important families.
Presiding over the body was the reigning
high priest.

The Council
acted as a kind of national high court.
It had its own police and power of arrest.
This is the Council that arrested Jesus.

*The Talmud describes the council
as sitting in a semicircle. . . .
Sentence could not be passed
except on the testimony of two witnesses.
A sentence of acquittal
could be pronounced on the same day,
but a conviction could not be pronounced
until the following day.
Each member
voted by rising in the sight of all,
beginning with the youngest.*

A simple majority was sufficient for acquittal,
but a conviction
required a majority of two.

It was before this group
that Peter and John were brought
and questioned about their actions.

Peter, full of the Holy Spirit,
answered them,
"Leaders of the people and elders:
if we are being questioned today
about the good deed done to the lame man
and how he was healed,
then you should all know,
and all the people of Israel should know,
that this man stands here before you
completely well through the power
of the name of Jesus Christ of Nazareth—
whom you crucified and whom God raised
from death. . . .
Salvation is to be found through him alone."

ACTS 4:8-12

Peter's boldness and eloquence
made a profound impression on the Council.
After deliberating in private,
the Council members
decided to take no disciplinary action.
Yet they felt it necessary to discourage
future public displays by Peter and John.

So they called them back in
and told them that under no condition
were they to speak
or to teach in the name of Jesus.
But Peter and John answered them,
"You yourselves judge
which is right in God's sight—
to obey you or to obey God.

What Happened to Me?

I'm a very logical, scientific-minded person.
I need proofs for everything.
Yet, something has happened to me
here in college that I can't explain rationally,
scientifically, or even psychologically.

I've become preoccupied with Jesus Christ,
who I somehow feel is working within me. . . .
I can't explain this feeling.
It came about mainly these past few months,
when I began reading about the early Christians.
I was so amazed and in awe of these people
that I found it impossible to question Jesus,
or doubt who he is—the son of God.

In short, I guess I began to believe
firmly and thoughtfully
what I was taught ever since I was a child.
I began to see what
the apostles and disciples saw and loved.
Jesus became real. . . .

I still have occasional doubts,
but there remains that unexplainable something
inside me, even in my doubts.
Call it crazy, psychotic, or whatever . . .
I can't explain it, nor does it go away,
nor did I induce it to come on.
It just happened.

Robert Rybicki

Agathos and *kalos*, William Barclay notes,
are two ancient Greek words for "good."
The first means "good only";
the second means
"not only good, but also looking good."

It was the second "goodness"
that radiated from the early Christians.
Genuine Christianity is an attractive thing.

What Makes a Witness?

When the Holy Spirit comes upon you,
you will be filled with power,
and you will be witnesses for me ...
to the ends of the earth.

ACTS 1:8

Witnesses exhibit three characteristics.

First, they speak from firsthand experience.
Thus John writes:

We have heard [the Word of life],
and we have seen it with our eyes ...
and our hands have touched it.

1 JOHN 1:1

Second, witnesses live for one thing
above all else: to proclaim their message.
Thus, F. B. Rhein writes of Jesus' followers:

Off they went with burning urgency
to tell the news to all the world.
Their lives were led for that end
and for that end alone.

Finally, witnesses are willing to die
for the message they proclaim.
Thus the Greeks used the same name, *martus*,
to designate both "witness" and "martyr."

For we cannot stop speaking
of what we ourselves have seen and heard."
So the Council warned them
even more strongly and then set them free.

ACTS 4:18–21

When Peter and John
reported back to the Christian community,
there was great alarm and concern.

All joined together in prayer to God. ...

When they finished praying,
the place where they were meeting
was shaken.
They were all filled with the Holy Spirit
and began to proclaim God's message
with boldness.

ACTS 4:24, 31

28

5
Light and Darkness

"Christian Commune . . ."
MICHAEL HIRSLEY

Dave and Neta Jackson,
standing beside a dining room table
that stretches the length of the room,
are part of a large family in Evanston. . . .

The Evanston group,
called Reba Place Fellowship, is 140 adults
and 100 children comprising an extended family,
living in a commune.

"All our members are
committed to sharing our lives as Christians
and to contributing our resources,
including all financial assets,
to a common purse," Jackson said. . . .

Reba has flourished 20 years
since it was founded by a small group
of Mennonite religious students
from Elkhart, Indiana. . . .

Each adult member
of Reba gets monthly allotments. . . .

If unusual medical expenses are incurred,
fellowships across the country lend help.
For example, Jackson said,
"We contribute to a commune in North Dakota
where a girl was seriously burned
and had medical bills of $70,000.
We always allocate part of our budget
to help others. . . ."

Major decisions . . .
are made at public meetings, Jackson said.
"The elders study proposed actions
and make recommendations," he said,
"but no action is taken
without public consensus.". . .
As member Lichtis put it,
". . . there has to be a lot of trust
among people who live together."

This contemporary effort to live out
the Gospel ideal of Christian community
was inspired, no doubt, by the idealized portrait
of the Christian community in Acts.
Consider this description, for example:

The group of believers
was one in mind and heart.
No one said that any of his belongings
was his own, but they all shared
with one another everything they had.
With great power the apostles gave witness
to the resurrection of the Lord Jesus,
and God poured rich blessings on them all.
There was no one in the group
who was in need.
Those who owned fields or houses
would sell them, bring the money received
from the sale, and turn it over to the apostles;
and the money was distributed to each one
according to his need.

ACTS 4:32-35

Luke's point is clear.
Jesus intended his followers to be
a "light" to the world, just as he was (John 9:5).
Matthew's presentation of the Sermon on the Mount
leaves no doubt about Jesus' mind on this.

29

Jesus saw the crowds
and went up a hill, where he sat down.
His disciples gathered around him,
and he began to teach them. . . .

"You are like salt for all mankind.
But if salt loses its saltiness,
there is no way to make it salty again.
It has become worthless, so it is thrown out
and people trample on it.

"You are like light for the whole world.
A city built on a hill cannot be hid.
No one lights a lamp and puts it under a bowl;
instead he puts it on the lampstand,
where it gives light for everyone in the house.
In the same way your light must shine
before people, so that they will see
the good things you do
and praise your Father in heaven."

MATTHEW 5:1-2, 13-16

CLAY SHOES

It is against this understanding
of Christian community
that we should read the vivid story
of Ananias and Sapphira.
Luke introduces it this way:

Joseph, a Levite born in Cyprus, . . .
sold a field he owned, brought the money,
and turned it over to the apostles.

But there was a man named Ananias,
who with his wife Sapphira
sold some property that belonged to them.
But with his wife's agreement
he kept part of the money for himself
and turned the rest over to the apostles.

ACTS 4:36-5:2

Somehow Peter learned of the deception
and confronted Ananias about it.

Total Dedication

A Communist youth
wrote in a letter some years ago:

Presbyterian Survey
COMMUNIST YOUTH

I can't carry on a friendship,
a love affair, or even a conversation
without relating it to this force
which both drives and guides my life. . . .

I have already
been in jail because of my ideas. . . .
I am ready to go before a firing squad.

A certain percentage of us get killed. . . .
Life is no bed of roses.
A genuine radical lives in virtual poverty.
He turns back to the party
every penny he makes above what
is absolutely necessary to keep him alive.

This same idealism
fueled the spirit of many early Christians.
It sprang, however, not from adherence
to a philosophy or dedication to a party
but from adherence to the Gospel
and dedication to a person.

"Before you sold the property,
it belonged to you;
and after you sold it, the money was yours.
Why, then, did you decide to do such a thing?
You have not lied to men—
you have lied to God!"
As soon as Ananias heard this,
he fell down dead;
and all who heard about it were terrified.

ACTS 5:4-5

History records similar happenings.
The story is told, for example,
that King Edward I raged so violently at a courtier
that the man dropped dead from fright.

Regardless of how one might interpret
the death of Ananias, Luke's reason
for narrating the story should not be lost.
It dramatizes the gravity of a sin
not only against the ideal of Christian community,
but against the Holy Spirit as well.
One writer says of Ananias:

His first fault has been
a proud and false assertion of generosity.
This sin has led him and his wife
into an attempt to deceive the apostles,
a more serious sin.
For it is the equivalent of lying to the Spirit,
to God himself.

Luke follows the Ananias story with a summary.
This is a technique frequently used by him
in early Acts (2:42-47, 4:32-35, 5:12-16, 6:7).
It not only acts as a bridge
over informational gaps in his presentation
but also creates the desirable impression
of a continuous narrative. He writes:

Many miracles and wonders
were being performed among the people
by the apostles. . . .
As a result of what the apostles were doing,
sick people were carried out into the streets

Who Was the Angel?

"The Bible, the People's Book"
CARLOS MESTERS

When the poor read the Bible,
they are not trying to interpret it,
they are trying to interpret life
with the help of the Bible. . . .

This gives the poor a new way of seeing. . . .

Once, in Goias [Brazil],
we read the passage . . . when the angel of the Lord
came and freed the apostles from jail.
The pastoral worker asked his people:
"Who was the angel?"

One of the women present
gave this answer: "Oh, I know.
When Bishop Pedro Casaldaliga
was attacked in his house
and the police surrounded it with machine guns,
no one could get in or out
and no one knew what was going on.
A little girl sneaked in without being seen,
got a message from Dom Pedro,
ran to the airport and hitched a ride
to Goiana where the bishops were meeting.
They got the message, made a big fuss
and Dom Pedro was set free.
So that little girl was the angel of the Lord!"

and placed on beds and mats
so that at least Peter's shadow might fall
on some of them as he passed by.
And crowds of people came in from the towns
around Jerusalem,
bringing those who were sick
or who had evil spirits in them;
and they were all healed.

ACTS 5:12-16

LIGHTNING BOLT

The excitement generated by such cures
was exactly what the Jewish Council feared.

Then
the High Priest and all his companions,
members of the local party of the Sadducees,
became extremely jealous of the apostles;
so they decided to take action.
They arrested the apostles and put them
in the public jail.
But that night an angel of the Lord
opened the prison gates, led the apostles out,
and said to them,
"Go and stand in the Temple,
and tell the people all about this new life."
The apostles obeyed, and at dawn
they entered the Temple and started teaching.

ACTS 5:17-21

Today we are inclined to ask
how we should interpret "angel of the Lord."

Angels are, above all,
"God's messengers" or "instruments."
The Bible portrays them as taking many forms.
For example, Isaiah 37:36 says
the Lord's "angel" struck the Assyrian army.
Describing the same event,
Sirach 48:21,
in the original Greek text,
says a "plague" struck the army.

The "jailbreak"
did not have to occur in a "marvelous" way.
An unexpected, friendly jailer
might have served as the "angel of the Lord."

The reaction of the Council was predictable.
The apostles were rearrested.
Again the High Priest confronted them.

"We gave you strict orders
not to teach in the name of this man . . .
but see what you have done!"

ACTS 5:28

THE DEFENSE

The apostles responded exactly as they did
on the previous occasion, saying:

"We must obey God, not men.
The God of our ancestors raised Jesus . . .
to his right side as Leader and Savior,
to give the people of Israel the opportunity
to repent and have their sins forgiven.
We are witnesses to these things—
we and the Holy Spirit,
who is God's gift to those who obey him."

ACTS 5:29-32

History honors a parade of people
who chose the course the apostles chose—
to obey God, not human beings.

For example, during the Mexican War,
Henry David Thoreau went to jail
rather than pay a tax
he thought was being used to wage a war
to expand slave-holding territories.

His friend Emerson, a slavery opponent too,
heard of Thoreau's confinement.
Visiting him, Emerson inquired gently:
"Henry, why are you here?"

ר לאהלא יברדי גלאל ה

ραβιΓαμελιΛ

Tomb Inscription

Gamaliel was Paul's teacher (Acts 22:3)
and the son
of a founder of the Pharisee party.

In the spirit and tradition of his father,
Gamaliel counseled moderation
toward the apostles.

Gamaliel II, Gamaliel's grandson,
became president of the Sanhedrin,
as did his grandson Judah I.

The latter was also editor of the Mishnah,
a book of rabbinical teachings.

Gamaliel III, Judah's son,
succeeded his famous father
as president of the Sanhedrin.

Against this backdrop,
the inscription in Hebrew and Greek, above,
generates a rich flood of memories.
It was found in a cave at Beth She'arim,
an ancient Jewish burial place.

Thoreau's retort became the classic reply
of the fully committed person
to the partially committed person:
"Waldo, why are you *not* here?"

It is not easy to stand up and be counted
when the crunch of conscience comes.
Jesus cautioned candidly:

*"Do not be afraid of those
who kill the body but cannot kill the soul. . . .
If anyone declares publicly that he belongs
to me, I will do the same for him
before my Father in heaven.*

*But if anyone rejects me publicly,
I will reject him before my Father in heaven."*
                                    MATTHEW 10:28–33

The reaction of the Jewish Council members
to the apostles' statement was predictable.
They interpreted the statement as having
not only the ring of religious heresy
but also the ring of political rebellion.
For the good of their religion,
and for the sake of their nation,
they saw only one course of action open.
These men and their "Jesus movement"
had to be stopped.
Otherwise, complete chaos would result.

33

Was Luke Wrong?

"Theudas appeared some time ago.
But he was killed, all his followers
were scattered, and his movement died out."

ACTS 5:36

The Jewish historian Josephus
puts the Theudas movement around A.D. 45,
some ten years *after* Gamaliel's speech.
Some scholars cite this as a classic case
where Luke erred in reconstructing a speech.

Other scholars take a "wait-and-see" posture.
They remind us that experts also accused Luke
of error when he spoke of *politarchs*
("city authorities") in Acts 17:6.
Later, archaeologists unearthed inscriptions
proving Luke was absolutely correct.
One defender of Luke says this:

The Acts of the Apostles
WILLIAM BARCLAY

In those days Palestine had
a quick succession of fire-brand leaders. . . .
Who this Theudas was we do not know.
There was a Theudas some years later
who led a band of people out to the Jordan
with the promise
that he would divide the waters
and they would walk over dryshod,
and whose rising was swiftly dealt with.
Theudas was a common name and no doubt
this was just such another fire-brand.

In any event,
Luke's point in the Gamaliel speech is clear:
let history be the judge
of Jesus and his movement.

Historian's Verdict

The Council took Gamaliel's advice
and decided to let history be the judge.
It is interesting that 2,000 years later,
H. G. Wells, a prominent historian
with no particular religious bent,
nominated Jesus as history's greatest man.

"The Three Greatest Men in History"
H. G. WELLS

I am speaking of him as a man. . . .
The historian must treat him as a man
just as the painter must paint him as a man. . . .

Of course the reader and I live in countries
where to millions of persons,
Jesus is more than a man.
But the historian must disregard that fact. . . .

The historian's test of an individual's greatness
is "What did he leave to grow?"
Did he start men thinking along fresh lines
with a vigor that persisted after him?
By this test Jesus stands first.

THE VERDICT

When the situation
was on the verge of erupting like a volcano,
Gamaliel, a respected Pharisee, stood up.

He ordered the apostles to be taken out . . .
and then he said to the Council,
"Fellow Israelites,
be careful what you do to these men.
You remember that Theudas appeared
some time ago, claiming to be somebody great,
and about four hundred men joined him.
But he was killed, all his followers
were scattered, and his movement died out.
After that, Judas the Galilean appeared
during the time of the census;
he drew a crowd after him,
but he also was killed, and all his followers
were scattered.
And so in this case, I tell you,
do not take any action against these men.
Leave them alone!
If what they have planned and done
is of human origin, it will disappear,
but if it comes from God,
you cannot possibly defeat them.
You could
find yourselves fighting against God!"

ACTS 5:34–39

For the time being
an explosive situation was defused.

6

New Wineskins

The story is told that Oliver Cromwell,
the great English general and statesman,
hired an artist to do his portrait.
When the painting was completed,
Cromwell saw that the artist had omitted
some warts from his face.
Cromwell told the artist to correct
the well-intentioned omissions, saying:
"Paint me, warts and all."

The portrait of the early church in Acts
clearly has its idealized dimensions,
but Luke also included a few "warts."

There was a quarrel
between Greek-speaking Jews and native Jews.
The Greek-speaking Jews claimed
that their widows were being neglected
in the daily distribution of funds.
So the twelve apostles
called the whole group of believers together
and said,
"It is not right for us
to neglect the preaching of God's word
in order to handle finances.
So then, brothers,
choose seven men among you who are known
to be full of the Holy Spirit and wisdom,

and we will put them in charge of this matter.
We ourselves, then, will give our full time
to prayer and the work of preaching."

ACTS 6:1–4

So the group chose seven men
to oversee the community's practical matters.

The group presented them to the apostles,
who prayed and placed their hands on them.

ACTS 6:6

The daily "distribution" *(diakonia)*
was now in the hands of "the seven."
Luke does not call them deacons,
but he does use the word *diakonia* twice
in referring to them.

This has led some to speculate
that "the seven" may have been
the church's first deacons.

The Acts of the Apostles
NEAL M. FLANAGAN

Luke's purpose here is not to record
the institution of the diaconate in a technical
sense, but to introduce this important group,
the Hellenists, and in particular Stephen. . . .

The appearance of Stephen and the Hellenists
marks the end of Christianity's first phase. . . .
So far the Church had remained moored
to the Temple and to the homes
of Judeo Christians in Jerusalem.
Now its horizon widens.

LEAVING THE COCOON

Thus the first confrontation
between Hebrew and Hellenistic Christians
ended not in disaster but in growth.
It led to the first of a series of steps
that saw the first Christian community,

The "Writing" Story

Our word *paper* comes from *papyrus,*
a reedlike plant that grew along the Nile.
These plants produced the "paper"
of the ancient world.
The process of turning the 15-foot stalks
into writing material is described by Pliny
in his *Natural History*.

Stalks were split lengthwise into thin strips.
One set of strips was arranged vertically;
a second set, horizontally, over the first set.
The two sets
were then moistened with water from the Nile,
which when muddy had a gluelike quality.
Then the two sets were pressed together,
dried in the sun,
and rubbed smooth with a flat stone.

Sheets could be cut to any desired size.
They could be stacked one on top of the other
to form a codex ("book").
Or sheets could be glued end to end
and rolled into a scroll.
The largest known scroll
is from the reign of Rameses II of Egypt.
It is 133 feet long and 17 inches wide.

Scribes wrote on the sheets or scrolls
with a tiny dried reed
whose point was shredded to form a brush.
Early scribes of the Bible
wrote without sentence breaks, punctuation,
or chapter divisions.

Chapter divisions
were created by scholars in the 13th century.
Verse divisions, to facilitate reference,
were added in the 16th century.

These ancient Egyptian figures
are gathering and splitting
papyrus stalks.

Time Bridge

Archaeologists uncovered this cornerstone
on Ophel Hill, just south of Jerusalem.
Some experts link it
to the Freedmen's synagogue of Acts 6:9.
The synagogue's congregation
was made up of descendants of Jews
who had been freed
after being prisoners of war,
apparently under Pompey in 63 B.C.
The inscription reads:

Theodotus, son of Vettenus,
priest and synagogue ruler,
son of a synagogue ruler,
grandson of a synagogue ruler,
built the synagogue
for the reading of the law
and for the teaching of the commandments,
and the guest-house and rooms
and cisterns of water
as a lodging for those from abroad
who need them—
which synagogue his fathers,
elders, and Simonides founded.

guided by the Holy Spirit,
adapt its structure and its leadership
so that it could carry out more effectively
the mission Jesus had given it.

From another viewpoint,
it led to the first of a series of steps
by which Christianity freed itself totally
from the structures and institutions of Judaism.

In short,
it led to the development of fresh wineskins
for the new wine of Christianity.
Jesus had said:

"No one patches up an old coat
with a piece of new cloth,
for the new patch will shrink
and make an even bigger hole in the coat.
Nor does anyone
pour new wine into used wineskins,
for the skins will burst,
the wine will pour out,
and the skins will be ruined.
Instead,
new wine is poured into fresh wineskins,
and both will keep in good condition."

MATTHEW 9:16–17

Thus the first confrontation
between Hebrew and Hellenistic Christians
began a process by which Christianity
broke out of its confining cocoon,
stretched its young wings,
and embraced a wider world.

7

Vulnerable Hero

For years, Westerns enjoyed
widespread popularity on TV screens.

Some traced their popularity to the ideal
of self-reliance they projected so appealingly.
The hero rode in from nowhere,
set things right, and rode back into nowhere.
He was a man alone, unattached, self-reliant.

Others said Westerns appealed to us
because they projected a savior-hero image
that made us feel good.
The champion in the white hat righted wrongs,
defended the innocent, and protected the weak.

As time wore on, new heroes appeared:
nurses, doctors, teachers, law enforcers.
They, too, saved people: the sick patient,
the exploited adult, the brutalized child.

But unlike history's true savior-heroes—
Socrates, Joan of Arc, Gandhi, King—
TV savior-heroes never get hurt.
After a few scuffles and minor setbacks,
they emerge victorious.
Their shining armor is never bent or dented,
only smudged.

Serious critics scoff at TV savior-heroes.
They are shallow, invulnerable.

Because of this, they do not serve us well.
They reinforce the error that saving people
and combating evil can be done successfully
without personal sacrifice or tragedy.

In sharp contrast to the TV savior-heroes
stand the heroes of early Christianity.
They were vulnerable; they suffered severely;
they paid for their beliefs with their lives.
Such a hero
was the first Christian martyr, Stephen.

Stephen was one of "the seven,"
chosen to direct the distribution of goods
among the first Christians.
Acts describes him in highly idealized terms.

Stephen, a man richly blessed by God
and full of power, performed great miracles
and wonders among the people.
But he was opposed by some men
who were members
of the synagogue of the Freedmen....
They seized Stephen
and took him before the Council.
Then they brought in some men
to tell lies about him.
"This man," they said, "is always talking
against our sacred Temple
and the Law of Moses...."

The High Priest asked Stephen,
"Is this true?"

ACTS 6:8–7:1

STEPHEN'S RESPONSE

Stephen began his defense by tracing
the history of God's dealings with Israel.
He began with God's call to Abraham
to leave his homeland and set out for
a new land which God would show to him.
Abraham obeyed.

This old Roman gate outside Tarsus,
birthplace of Saul (Paul),
recalls the massive walls
that once enclosed cities like Jerusalem.
Through such a gate
Stephen was driven and stoned (Acts 7:58).

Then Stephen recalled the birth of Isaac,
Abraham's son, and the birth of Isaac's son,
Jacob.
Jacob's name was changed to Israel by God,
and his 12 sons became the forerunners
of the 12 tribes of Israel, the Israelites.

Next Stephen recalled how one of the 12 sons,
Joseph, was betrayed by his brothers.
Later this rejected and persecuted brother
became the savior of the others (Acts 7:9-16).

Then Stephen recalled the enslavement
of the Israelites by the Egyptians.
God took pity on them
and raised up Moses to be their leader.
When still a young man,

Moses was rejected by some fellow Israelites
and forced to flee to the desert (Acts 7:20-29).
God used the rejection to prepare Moses
for his task ahead.
Stephen told how God spoke openly to Moses.

"'I have seen
the cruel suffering of my people in Egypt.
I have heard their groans,
and I have come down to set them free.
Come now; I will send you to Egypt.'...

"[Moses] led the people out of Egypt,
performing miracles and wonders....

"But our ancestors refused to obey him;
they pushed him aside

and wished that they could go back to Egypt. . . .
It was then that they made an idol
in the shape of a bull."

ACTS 7:34-41

Finally Stephen recalled
how God led Israel into the promised land.
Then Stephen paused,
looked right at the Council, and said:

"You are just like your ancestors: you too
have always resisted the Holy Spirit! . . .
They killed God's messengers,
who long ago announced the coming
of his righteous Servant.
And now you have betrayed and murdered him.
You are the ones who received God's law . . .
yet you have not obeyed it!"

As the members of the Council listened
to Stephen, they became furious. . . .
But Stephen, full of the Holy Spirit,
looked up to heaven and saw God's glory
and Jesus standing at the right side of God.
"Look!" he said.
"I see heaven opened and the Son of Man
standing at the right side of God!"

With a loud cry the Council members
covered their ears with their hands.
Then they all rushed at him at once,
threw him out of the city, and stoned him.
The witnesses left their cloaks
in the care of a young man named Saul.
They kept on stoning Stephen
as he called out to the Lord,
"Lord Jesus, receive my spirit!"
He knelt down and cried out in a loud voice,
"Lord! Do not remember this sin against them!"
He said this and died.

And Saul approved of his murder.

ACTS 7:51-8:1

The Council's reaction
was not that of an undisciplined mob.
On the contrary, the Council interpreted
Stephen's remarks as blasphemy,
and the law spelled out
how a blasphemer must be treated.

"Show him no mercy or pity,
and do not protect him. Kill him!
Be the first to stone him,
and then let everyone else stone him too.
Stone him to death!"

DEUTERONOMY 13:8-10

Stephen's last words,
"Do not remember this sin against them!"
show that as in life, so in death,
he tried to follow the example of his Master
(Luke 23:34, 46).

MEDITATION

The story of Stephen's death ends
with our attention shifting
from the bleeding youth on the ground
to an approving youth on the sidelines.
And as we internalize this scene,
we are left with an assortment of thoughts.

One thought
was expressed by Augustine this way:
"The church owes Saul to Stephen's prayer."

A second thought
is that of Tertullian, who said:
"The blood of martyrs
is the seed of the church."

Finally, Dostoevski observed:
"Men reject their prophets and slay them,
but they love their martyrs
and honor those whom they have slain."

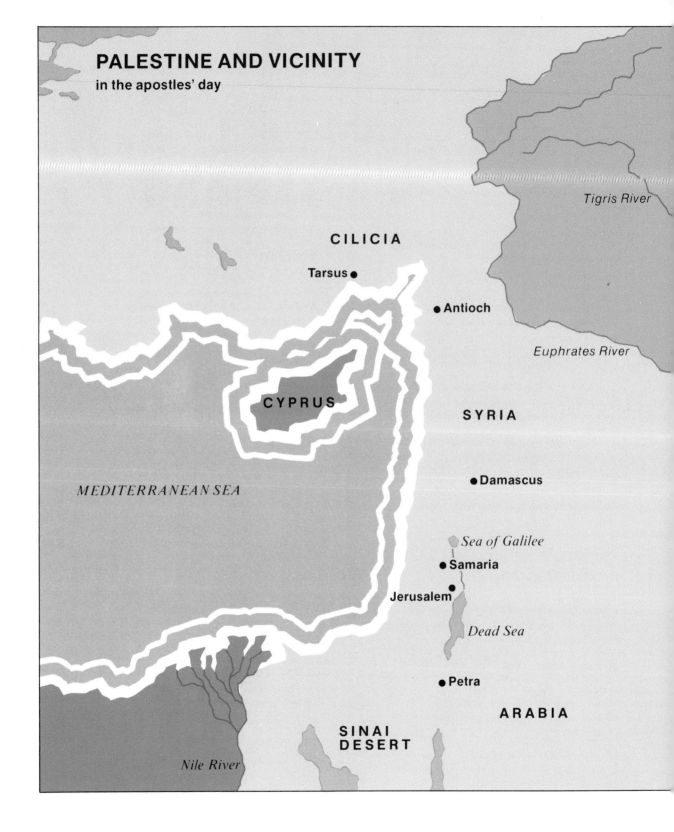

PALESTINE AND VICINITY
in the apostles' day

Tigris River

CILICIA

Tarsus ●

● Antioch

Euphrates River

CYPRUS

SYRIA

MEDITERRANEAN SEA

● Damascus

Sea of Galilee

● Samaria

Jerusalem ●

Dead Sea

● Petra

SINAI
DESERT

ARABIA

Nile River

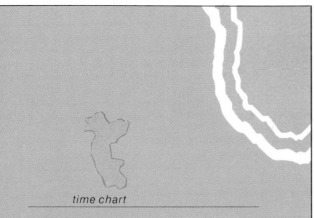

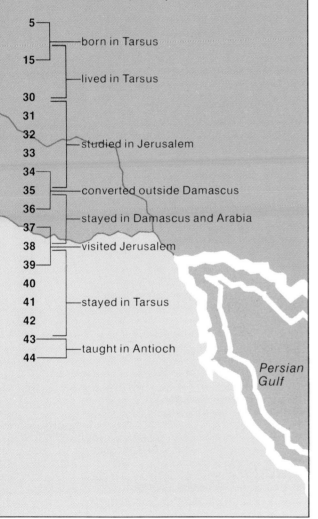

time chart

LIFE OF PAUL

before first journey

- 5
- born in Tarsus
- 15
- lived in Tarsus
- 30
- 31
- 32
- studied in Jerusalem
- 33
- 34
- 35 — converted outside Damascus
- 36
- 37
- stayed in Damascus and Arabia
- 38 — visited Jerusalem
- 39
- 40
- 41 — stayed in Tarsus
- 42
- 43
- 44 — taught in Antioch

Persian Gulf

PART TWO

JUDEA AND SAMARIA

Acts 8-12

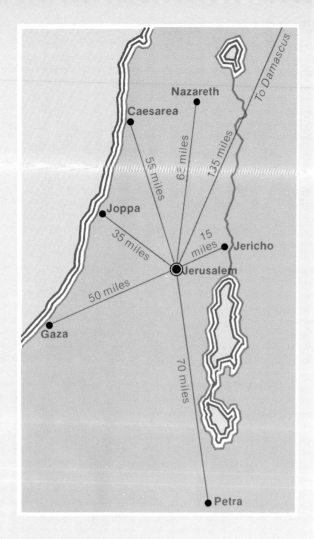

Ancient Travel

Ancient travel was normally done on foot,
and a trip lasted a number of days.
To prevent what happened to the man
in Jesus' parable of the Good Samaritan,
travel was usually done in caravans.

The map above
shows the distances in "air miles."
"Road miles" were greater
due to curves around hills.
For example, the distance traveled
from Jerusalem to Jericho
by the man in Jesus' parable
was about 20 miles.

Deafening Explosion

The stoning of Stephen
touched off a chain reaction of "explosions,"
whose sound echoed and echoed
until it was heard around the world.

All the believers,
except the apostles, were scattered
throughout the provinces of Judea
and Samaria. . . .
The believers who were scattered
went everywhere, preaching the message.

ACTS 8:1, 4

Thus began,
unplanned and seemingly by accident,
the second phase of Jesus' commission
to his apostles.

"When the Holy Spirit comes upon you,
you will be filled with power,
and you will be witnesses for me
in Jerusalem,
in all of Judea and Samaria,
and to the ends of the earth."

ACTS 1:8

PHILIP

The witness to Samaria was begun
by another young hero in the early church,
Philip (Acts 6:5).

H. V. Morton's unforgettable passage
in *In the Steps of St. Paul*
applies to this ancient Samaritan site.

"I cannot understand how a traveller . . .
can see a Corinthian capital lying in the mud
without feeling that such things hold a lesson
and a warning and, perhaps, a prophesy."

Philip went to the principal city in Samaria
and preached the Messiah to the people there.
The crowds
paid close attention to what Philip said,
as they listened to him
and saw the miracles that he performed.
Evil spirits
came out from many people with a loud cry,
and many paralyzed and lame people
were healed.
So there was great joy in that city.

ACTS 8:5-8

Once again, the power
that was present in Jesus during his lifetime
showed itself to be present in Jesus' followers.
The young church
extended the person and the mission of Jesus
into space and time to all peoples of all nations.

From a historical point of view,
the Samaritan breakthrough was remarkable
because of the 700-year-long hatred
that existed between Jews and Samaritans.

It began when invading Assyrian armies
conquered the northern kingdom of Israel,
of which Samaria was a part.
The invaders deported many Samaritans
but allowed some to remain behind.
Foreigners were brought in by the Assyrians
to occupy the land and property
left behind by the deported Samaritans.

In time, the Samaritans who remained behind
mingled and intermarried with the foreigners.
This situation infuriated southern Jews,
who regarded it as religious compromise.

As years passed,
the hostility heated up and intensified.
Jews banned Samaritans from the temple
and from all synagogues.

Their religious contributions were refused;
their testimony in courts was outlawed.
Eventually, Jews severed all communication
with Samaritans (John 4:9).

Samaritans, on the other hand, retaliated.
They made common cause with Jewish enemies.
They banned Jews from their towns (Luke 9:53).

Jesus reached out to the Samaritans (John 4:9).
He also challenged Jewish attitudes
toward Samaritans (Luke 10:33; 17:16).

When Philip announced the news
of Jesus' resurrection to the Samaritans,
he merely followed in the missionary footsteps
of Jesus.

Excited audiences
once cheered performances under the stars
in this ancient theater in Samaria.
Herod the Great (37 B.C.–A.D. 4) embellished
Samaria and renamed the city Sebaste (Augusta)
in honor of his Roman emperor.

He reached out to those people
whom traditional Jews considered
as having put themselves outside the pale
of God's loving embrace.

Word of Philip's success in Samaria
brought Peter and John to visit the area
and see for themselves the new development
taking place in the church.

When they arrived,
they prayed for the believers
that they might receive the Holy Spirit.
For the Holy Spirit
had not yet come down on any of them;
they had only been baptized
in the name of the Lord Jesus.
Then Peter and John
placed their hands on them,
and they received the Holy Spirit.

ACTS 8:15–17

By prayer and the laying on of hands,
Peter and John confirmed the new Christians,
sharing with them the gift of the Spirit
which they themselves received on Pentecost.

After they had given their testimony
and proclaimed the Lord's message,
Peter and John went back to Jerusalem.
On their way they preached the Good News
in many villages in Samaria.

ACTS 8:25

ETHIOPIAN CONVERT

The Holy Spirit continued
to bless and guide the preaching of Philip.
One day he encountered an "important official
in charge of the treasury of the queen of Ethiopia"
(Acts 8:27).
The official had been to Jerusalem to worship
and was returning home.

46

Philip heard him reading the prophet Isaiah
at the place where the prophet says:

*"He was like a sheep
that is taken to be slaughtered. . . .
He did not say a word."*

ACTS 8:32

Philip asked the official if he understood
the words of the prophet.

*The official replied,
"How can I understand unless someone
explains it to me?" . . .*

*Then Philip began to speak;
starting from this passage of scripture,
he told him the Good News about Jesus.*

ACTS 8:31, 36

When Philip finished with his instruction,
the official believed and was baptized.

In Philip's day,
there were many Gentiles in many nations
who were weary of the various gods
and the widespread superstitions of the time.
These Gentiles were attracted to Judaism,
with its one God, high moral code,
and noble style of religious worship.

Often such Gentiles attended synagogues
and followed certain basic Jewish observances.
Some of them were eventually converted,
accepting Judaism completely.
These were called *proselytes.*

More often than not, however,
such Gentiles merely frequented synagogues
to pray and to hear the Scriptures read.
They were never converted completely.
These Gentiles were called *God-fearers.*

Evidently, the Ethiopian fell into this group.

Occult Figure

Magazine stores
carry a variety of journals about such things
as astrology, fortune-telling, and the occult.
These journals take seriously
the claims that Hitler consulted the stars
and that Kennedy was warned about Dallas.

Fortune-telling, astrology, and the occult
were popular in Philip's time, also.
An occult figure popular among the Samaritans
was a man named Simon.

*They paid attention to him because . . .
he had astonished them with his magic.
But when they believed Philip's message
about the good news . . .
they were baptized, both men and women.
Simon himself also believed;
and after being baptized,
he stayed close to Philip and was astounded
when he saw the great wonders and miracles
that were being performed.*

ACTS 8:11–13

When Peter and John
conferred the Holy Spirit upon the Samaritans,
Simon slipped back to his old ways.

*He offered money to Peter and John,
and said, "Give this power to me too. . . ."*

*But Peter answered him,
"May you and your money go to hell,
for thinking that you can buy God's gift. . . .
Your heart is not right in God's sight.
Repent . . . and pray to the Lord
that he will forgive you."*

ACTS 8:18–22

What happened to Simon we are not told.
But to this day, the sin of trying to buy
spiritual gifts gets its name from him—simony.

47

9
Blinding Light

British newspaperman Douglas Hyde
couldn't stomach Christianity.
That's why he was reading Avro Manhattan's
*The Catholic Church
Against the Twentieth Century.*
It was one of the sources he was consulting
to prepare an article to denounce the church.

Yet, in a matter of months,
Douglas Hyde became a Christian himself.
He writes:

I Believed
DOUGLAS HYDE

*Instead of gaining ammunition
against the Church from Manhattan's book
I learned, despite tendentious writing,
something of the Church's social teaching.
It was written to make anti-Catholics.
It helped to make me "pro" instead.*

UNEXPECTED TURNABOUT

In the stormy days after Jesus' crucifixion,
another man became a Christian in a strange way.
He, too, had been an active opponent of Christ.
In fact, he had accepted a commission
to hunt down Christians
and bring them in for public interrogation.

One day this man, Saul of Tarsus,
was going to Damascus for this purpose.

*Suddenly
a light from the sky flashed around him.
He fell to the ground
and heard a voice saying to him,
"Saul, Saul! Why do you persecute me?"*

"Who are you, Lord?" he asked.

*"I am Jesus, whom you persecute,"
the voice said.
"But get up and go into the city,
where you will be told what you must do."*

*The men who were traveling with Saul
had stopped, not saying a word;
they heard the voice but could not see anyone.
Saul got up from the ground
and opened his eyes, but could not see a thing.
So they took him by the hand
and led him into Damascus.
For three days he was not able to see,
and during that time
he did not eat or drink anything.*

ACTS 9:3-9

WHAT HAPPENED

Few mystical experiences
are better known and more discussed
than Paul's Damascus road experience.
People ask: "What did Paul experience?
Did he have a vision? Did he see Jesus?"

This East Gate of modern Damascus
rests on the exact spot
as did the gate of Paul's time.
It leads through to the street called "Straight."

Early Sites of Christianity
PETER BAMM

If Stones Talked

Jet aircraft
scream in and out of the Damascus airport,
carrying tourists from all parts of the world.
The Arab-controlled capital of Syria
has spilled over
far beyond the city walls that Paul knew.
Yet, some things about the famous city
have not changed in 2,000 years.

The ancient street called "Straight"
still funnels traffic
on an east-west axis through Damascus.
The East Gate has been rebuilt
but still stands where it did in Paul's time.
If you look closely,
you can still see stones from the old wall
keeping silent vigil in the new wall.

*These stones
have seen a thousand sights since the day
when Paul was struck with blindness.
They have seen
the arrogance of triumphant armies
and the tears of the defeated.
Innumerable caravans
have passed through this gate,
bringing silks and incense,
the valuables of the East. . . .
These stones have seen the cart
with the million pieces of gold
with which the Damascenes ransomed themselves
from Tamerlane, the Mongol Khan.*

But none of these sights
compares to that of a pathetic blind man
stumbling through the gate, led by a guide.
The blind man, of course, is Paul—
still confused and still reeling
from the experience that would revolutionize
not only his own life but all history.

49

A Bedouin (nomadic desert dweller) leads his horse through the narrow Siq that links ancient Petra with the outside world. The city was part of the Nabataean kingdom, which declined steadily after trade routes bypassed Petra in the early first century A.D.

The tiny figure, visible in the opening, gives some idea of the immensity of the so-called Deir, a giant tomb carved into the mountainside.

Lost City

Small wonder no one saw it.
The entrance to the canyon city
was a narrow Siq ("pass")
that was a mile or so long.
At times the Siq narrowed to three feet.
In places it soared 300 feet skyward.

John Burckhardt stood spellbound.
As far as the Swiss explorer could see
was a city of hundreds of structures—

not made of wood, concrete, or stone,
but "carved" from the canyon walls.

This was Petra, a Nabataean city,
which until August 12, 1812,
no Western person had ever laid eyes on.

A fourth-century earthquake wrecked the city,
turning it into a ghost town.

Undoubtedly, Paul walked through the pass
and visited Petra during his Arabian sojourn.

Two ancient cliff carvings
cut into the stone cliffs
of Petra

Elsewhere, Paul describes the experience
as a "vision I had from heaven" (Acts 26:19).
Elsewhere, also, he describes it
as an "appearance" of Jesus (1 Corinthians 15:8).
Perhaps, however, even Paul himself
was hard pressed to know what happened.
He makes that clear in another passage
concerning this or a different experience.
Referring to himself in the third person, he says:

I know a certain Christian man
who fourteen years ago
was snatched up to the highest heaven
(I do not know
whether this actually happened or whether
he had a vision—only God knows).

2 CORINTHIANS 12:2

Regardless of what took place,
this much is clear: Paul was a changed man.
He expected to gallop into Damascus
with his usual power and authority.
Instead, he groped into the city,
clinging like a child to a guide's hand.

DARK DAYS AHEAD

There was a Christian in Damascus
named Ananias.
He had a vision, in which the Lord
said to him, "Ananias!"

"Here I am, Lord," he answered.

The Lord said to him,
"Get ready and go to Straight Street,
and at the house of Judas ask for a man
from Tarsus named Saul. . . .

"Go, because I have chosen him to serve me,
to make my name known to Gentiles
and kings and to the people of Israel. . . ."

51

So Ananias went, entered the house
where Saul was, and placed his hands on him.

At once something like fish scales
fell from Saul's eyes,
and he was able to see again.
He stood up and was baptized;
and after he had eaten,
his strength came back. . . .

He went straight to the synagogues
and began to preach
that Jesus was the Son of God.

All who heard him were amazed and asked,
"Isn't he the one who in Jerusalem
was killing those
who worship that man Jesus? . . ."

Saul's preaching became even more powerful,
and his proofs that Jesus was the Messiah
were so convincing that the Jews who lived
in Damascus could not answer him.

After many days had gone by,
the Jews met together and made plans
to kill Saul, but he was told of their plan.
Day and night they watched the city gates
in order to kill him.
But one night Saul's followers took him
and let him down through an opening
in the wall, lowering him in a basket.

ACTS 9:10–25

From Damascus,
Saul, also known as Paul (Acts 13:9),
went to Arabia (Galatians 1:17).
Arabia is that vast, desolate land
that stretches south below the Dead Sea.
Where Paul went or what he did in Arabia
is not mentioned anywhere in his writings.
One can only guess.

To some retreat on a near-by oasis
Paul must have gone,
to begin a tremendous inner reconstruction
of his religious thinking.
For he had not just lightly added Jesus
to his Jewish theology,
as the Messiah foretold by the prophets. . . .
The cornerstones
of his theology and practice
must be rigorously reexamined,
in the light of his new religious experience.
How drastically and honestly this was done
his letters still show.

This total restructuring
of Paul's understanding of Jewish scripture
and of Jewish tradition took shape, probably,
in some silent cave in the Arabian desert.

GREATER TRIALS

After his extended retreat in Arabia,
Paul returned to Damascus and, eventually,
to Jerusalem (Galatians 1:18).

In Jerusalem, serious trouble awaited him.
The Christians could not believe
that he had actually become one of them.

They were all afraid of him.
Then Barnabas came to his help
and took him to the apostles.
He explained to them how Saul
had seen the Lord on the road
and that the Lord had spoken to him.
He also told them how boldly Saul had
preached in the name of Jesus in Damascus.

52

And so Saul stayed with them
and went all over Jerusalem,
preaching boldly in the name of the Lord.
He also talked and disputed
with the Greek-speaking Jews,
but they tried to kill him.
When the believers found out about this,
they took Saul to Caesarea
and sent him away to Tarsus.

ACTS 9:26–30

As Paul was being removed from Jerusalem,
probably under the cover of darkness,
he must have wondered
about the strange turn of events.
He had made a tremendous conversion,
but no one would listen to him.

Perhaps, as he looked up at the stars,
he felt a strange new kinship with Abraham,
his father in the faith.
God had called him, too, and taken him
from his familiar surroundings and friends
without telling him why (Genesis 12:1).

Walk in Darkness

The mysterious pattern
that marked Paul's converted life
has marked the lives of many Christians.
God seems to call by stages,
not letting us see where he is leading us.
Here is an example.

Letters from the Desert
CARLO CARRETTO

Three times in my life
I have been aware of this [God's] call.

The first one brought about my conversion
when I was eighteen years old. . . .

From that day on I knew I was a Christian,
and was aware that a completely new life
had been opened up for me.

The second time, when I was twenty-three,
I was thinking of getting married. . . .
I heard the same voice . . .
"You will offer your life to me. . . ."

Then, when I was forty-four years old,
there occurred the most serious call of my life:
the call to the contemplative life.
I experienced it deeply. . . .

"Come with me into the desert.
It is not your acts and deeds I want;
I want your prayer, your love."

Carlo Carretto went into the desert.
And there he remains to this day,
leading a life of prayer and love
as a member of the Little Brothers of Jesus.

10 Turning Point

At one point in the Civil War,
morale among the Northern troops hit bottom.
Only one man could possibly rally them.
He was the man who had trained them
and for whom they still held a deep respect.

Thus it was that President Lincoln
turned to General McClellan in the crisis.
McClellan saddled his great black horse
and rode to Virginia.

This Hallowed Ground
BRUCE CATTON

*He cantered down the dusty roads
and he met the heads of the retreating columns,
and he cried words of encouragement
and swung his little cap,
and he gave the beaten men
what no other man alive could have given them—
enthusiasm, hope, confidence. . . .
Down mile after mile of Virginia roads
the stumbling columns came alive,
and threw caps and knapsacks into the air,
and yelled until they could yell no more . . .
because they saw this dapper little rider
outlined against the purple starlight.*

DM
L. MAGNIUS
FELIX
MIL LEG X FRET B TRIB
MIL ANN XVIII VIX XXXIX

Stones Speak

Archaeological evidence
relating to Roman soldiers, like Cornelius,
has survived the centuries.
This abbreviated-style inscription reads:

*Sacred to the Memory
L Magnius
Felix
Tenth Legion, Fretensis, orderly to a tribune
Eighteen years service; died age 39*

The Roman legions garrisoned in Judea
made their headquarters in Caesarea.
These included the cohort (regiment)
to which Cornelius belonged.

Cornelius had the rank of centurion (captain),
commanding a century (nominally 100 men).
Six centuries made up a cohort (nominally 600).
Ten cohorts made a legion (nominally 6,000),
commanded by a legate and six tribunes.

Tourists walk over the same ancient routes once traversed by Cornelius and his soldiers.

And this, in a way,
was the turning point of the war. . . .
And American history would be different
forever after.

CROSSROAD

Almost every great movement
can identify a turning point in its history—
an event that aimed it in the right direction
at the right time.

A major crossroad or turning point
in the history of Christianity
took place in the city of Caesarea-on-the-Sea.

Located on the Mediterranean Sea,
Caesarea was the seaside headquarters
of the Roman army stationed in Palestine.
One of the officers at Caesarea
was a centurion named Cornelius.

Commanding 100 soldiers, the centurion
was the backbone of the Roman army.

 The Acts of the Apostles
WILLIAM BARCLAY

An ancient historian describes
the qualifications of the centurion like this.
"Centurions are desired not to be overbold
and reckless so much as good leaders,
of steady and prudent mind,
not prone to take the offensive
to start fighting wantonly,
but able when overwhelmed and hard-pressed
to stand fast and die at their posts."

Cornelius was not only a centurion
but also a "religious man" (Acts 10:2).
The Greek expression this phrase translates
is a technical one: a "God-fearer,"
or a Gentile attracted to Judaism.

TWO VISIONS

One day Cornelius was at prayer
when an angel appeared to him and said:

"God is pleased with your prayers
and works of charity,
and is ready to answer you.
And now send some men to Joppa
for a certain man
whose full name is Simon Peter. . . ."

The next day, as they were on their way
and coming near Joppa,
Peter went up on the roof of the house
about noon in order to pray.
He became hungry and wanted something to eat;
while the food was being prepared,
he had a vision.
He saw heaven opened
and something coming down
that looked like a large sheet being lowered
by its four corners to the earth.

Shown here is a missionary, Reverend Frank Hoare,
baptizing in the Fiji Islands.
If his baptistry looks like a tomb,
that's just what it was intended to look like. Paul wrote:

"By our baptism . . . we were buried with [Christ]
and shared his death, in order that,
just as Christ was raised from death . . .
so also we might live a new life."

Romans 6:4

Bare Feet

A missionary in the Fiji Islands
found himself in a position similar
to the one Peter faced with the Gentiles.
Fiji Islanders are mostly Muslims and Hindus.
How do you present Christianity to people
who have a totally different background?

After praying over the question,
the young missionary, Reverend Frank Hoare,
decided to imitate the holy men of India.
He traveled among the people on foot.
His message was the Christmas story.
Most Fiji Islanders celebrated Christmas,
but few knew the reason why.

Barefooting it through sugarcane fields,
the young missionary
found open doors and open hearts.
The islanders accepted him as a holy man.
He said later:

To be received kindly, to laugh and to joke,
and still be able to speak
about what is closest to my heart
was a tremendous experience.

For those islanders who asked for baptism,
the missionary used total immersion.
This way of baptizing was more intelligible
to people who were accustomed
to seeking forgiveness from their sins
by washing in holy rivers, like the Ganges.

In it were all kinds of animals, reptiles,
and wild birds.
A voice said to him, "Get up, Peter; kill and eat!"

But Peter said, "Certainly not, Lord!
I have never eaten anything ritually unclean
or defiled."

The voice spoke to him again,
"Do not consider anything unclean
that God has declared clean."
This happened three times,
and then the thing was taken back up
into heaven.

ACTS 10:4-16

As Peter was pondering the vision,
the men sent by Cornelius arrived.
They told Peter about Cornelius's vision
and asked him to come to Cornelius's house.
Peter agreed.

The next day the party set out.
When they arrived at the house of Cornelius,
many Gentiles were waiting for Peter.

Peter began to speak:
"I now realize that it is true
that God treats everyone on the same basis.
Whoever fears him
and does what is right is acceptable to him,
no matter what race he belongs to."

ACTS 10:34-35

Peter then preached to them the Good News
about Jesus.

While Peter was still speaking,
the Holy Spirit came down on all those
who were listening to his message.
The Jewish believers
who had come to Joppa with Peter
were amazed that God had poured out
his gift of the Holy Spirit on the Gentiles also.

For they heard them speaking in strange
tongues and praising God's greatness.
Peter spoke up:
"These people have received the Holy Spirit,
just as we also did.
Can anyone, then, stop them
from being baptized with water?"
So he ordered them to be baptized
in the name of Jesus Christ.

ACTS 10:44-48

The Holy Spirit,
given to Jews in Jerusalem (Acts 2:4) and
half-Jews in Samaria (8:17), is now given
to God-fearing Gentiles in Caesarea.
Progressively,
the young church reaches out to all peoples.
Each "pentecost" is presided over by Peter.

News of this latest development
spread like a forest fire out of control.
When Jewish Christians in Jerusalem
heard about it, they were amazed.

Their initial enthusiasm, however,
was dampened when they heard
that Peter had entered the home of a Gentile.
No Jew could take it upon himself to do that.

Then came an even more shocking surprise.
They learned that Peter did not require
the new converts to be circumcised.
How could he permit such a situation?
Was not circumcision the sign
of God's covenant with his chosen people?

WHY ALL THIS?

When Peter returned to Jerusalem,
the Jewish Christians gathered to hear
what explanation he would give.

So Peter gave them a complete account
of what had happened from the beginning.

ACTS 11:4

When Peter came to the end,
describing the coming of the Holy Spirit
upon the Gentiles, he said:

"Then I remembered what the Lord had said:
'John baptized with water,
but you will be baptized with the Holy Spirit.'
It is clear that God gave those Gentiles
the same gift that he gave us
when we believed in the Lord Jesus Christ;
who was I, then, to try to stop God!"

When they heard this,
they stopped their criticism and praised God,
saying,
"Then God has given to the Gentiles also
the opportunity to repent and live!"

ACTS 11:16–18

NEW UNDERSTANDING

Peter's dramatic experience in Caesarea
was a turning point
in the history of early Christianity.
It gave the young church a new insight
into the full scope of God's kingdom.

The importance of this new understanding
is clear from the duplicate description
Luke gives to Peter's vision (10:9-16; 11:7-9)
and to Cornelius's vision (10:3-8, 30-33).

Few events in early Christian history
changed the course of the church's future—
even the future of the entire world—
as did this one.

Before this event,
Jewish Christians had not yet understood
fully the new identity they had been given
on Pentecost by the coming of the Spirit.

Excavations at Caesarea
include this outdoor amphitheater.
Sitting under the sky,
modern tourists watch evening performances
from the same reconstructed theater
to which soldiers like Cornelius came
for relaxation and entertainment.

The ancient amphitheater lay open
not only to the sky
but also to the gentle breezes of the sea.

This "pentecost of the Gentiles" demonstrated
that they were not just another religious party,
like the Pharisees, Sadducees, or Essenes.

They began to see that, like Jesus,
they were called to reach out to all peoples,
especially society's "second-class" citizens.
Above all this included the poor. Jesus said:

"Happy are you poor;
the Kingdom of God is yours!
Happy are you who are hungry now;
you will be filled!
Happy are you who weep now;
you will laugh!"

LUKE 6:20-21

Similarly,
there were the outcasts and the tax collectors.
Jesus defended his association with them, saying:

"People who are well do not need a doctor,
but only those who are sick.
I have not come
to call respectable people to repent, but outcasts."

LUKE 5:31-32

And there were the women.
Luke's Gospel portrays Jesus' special sensitivity
to them, citing four episodes not found
elsewhere in the Gospels (7:11-17; 8:1-3;
15:8-10; 18:1-8).

In short, as days stretched into weeks
and weeks stretched into months,
it became clearer to Jewish Christians
that they were a new creation.
Paul would eventually find the right words
to describe them: they were the "body of Christ"
extending the mission of Christ
into space and time.

59

11
Scattered Everywhere

This silver coin,
showing the head of Emperor Augustus Caesar,
was minted in Antioch
some years before Paul's arrival in the city.
It was probably still in circulation
when he taught there.

Dr. Charles Townes won the Nobel Prize
for his work on the laser and the maser.
One of his "breakthrough" insights
came accidentally,
while he was sitting quietly on a park bench
looking at flowers.

History shows
that many other discoveries and movements
owe their origin to apparent accidents,
rather than human design.

Such was the case, also,
of the first great missionary movement
in the early church.
Had Christians not been persecuted in Judea,
they might not have gone forth—
at least as early as they did—
to preach the Good News outside Judea.

THREE STAGES

The outbreak of persecution scattered
Jesus' followers, sending them everywhere.
Thus they continued
the step-by-step implementation
of Jesus' commission:

*"You will be witnesses for me in Jerusalem,
in all of Judea and Samaria,
and to the ends of the earth."*

ACTS 1:8

First, Philip instructed the Samaritans,
who were part Jew by race and by religion.
Next, Peter instructed Cornelius, a Gentile;
but it was Cornelius who took the initiative.
Finally, Christians took the initiative,
going directly to the Gentiles.

*Some of the believers
who were scattered by the persecution . . .*

went as far as Phoenicia, Cyprus, and Antioch,
telling the message to Jews only.
But other believers,
men from Cyprus and Cyrene,
went to Antioch and proclaimed the message
to Gentiles also. . . .
The Lord's power was with them,
and a great number of people believed
and turned to the Lord.

ACTS 11:19-21

When the news of this latest development
reached the church in Jerusalem,
"they sent Barnabas to Antioch" (Acts 11:22).

BARNABAS

Born on the island of Cyprus, Barnabas
was one of Christianity's first converts.
His name was originally Joseph,
but the apostles christened him Barnabas
(Acts 4:36).

Those who have studied
the various references to Barnabas in Acts
are not surprised that he was chosen
to oversee church activity in Antioch.

The Acts of the Apostles
F. J. FOAKES-JACKSON

Barnabas indeed
is one of the most attractive characters
in the New Testament. . . .
Probably inferior in ability to Paul,
he was his superior in Christian graces.
He seems to have been utterly without jealousy,
eager to excuse the faults of others,
quick to recognize merit,
ready to compromise for the sake of peace. . . .
The virtues of Barnabas
make him singularly lovable.

Buried City

A Turkish construction company
digging in modern Antakya might find itself
unearthing debris from ancient Antioch.
Fortunately, Antakya sits on only part
of the ancient city.
This makes it possible for archaeologists
to explore the buried city.

Princeton University digs have uncovered
everything from an ancient stadium to streets
that Paul and Barnabas may have walked.
They have also unearthed mosaic floors
and public baths.
The multicolored mosaic floors, especially,
give an insight into life in ancient Antioch.

This mosaic, excavated at Antioch,
celebrates Dionysus' victory over Heracles
in a drinking bout.

Where Paul Grew Up

Purple sails flap in the wind,
while silver oars stroke the cool water
to the gentle rhythm of flutes and harps.
This is how the Greek biographer Plutarch
describes Cleopatra, the Egyptian queen,
sailing up the Cydnus River to Tarsus.

As Cleopatra lounges on the deck,
crowds throng the riverbank to greet her.
Meanwhile, a cool Mark Antony sits alone
in the town square whistling to himself.

Paul's ancestors may have viewed the sight
and replayed it for the youthful Paul.

Other celebrities who visited Tarsus
included Julius Caesar and Augustus Caesar.
Strabo, the Greek geographer, says that
Tarsus was a center of culture and learning
that, in Paul's time, surpassed even Athens.
It is not surprising that Paul was proud
of his birthplace (Acts 21:39).

Because of the importance of Tarsus,
its people were granted Roman citizenship.
This citizenship saved Paul's life
more than once (Acts 22:25-29).

Like all Jewish boys,
Paul was taught a trade to earn a living.
He learned the art of "tent making,"
although the original Greek word
could also be translated as "leather working."
Paul worked at this trade,
even during his missionary days (Acts 18:3).

Paul left Tarsus
to study under the great Gamaliel (Acts 22:3).
He returned for a period
after his conversion to Christianity.

Falls on the Cydnus ("cold river") today.
The river's origin is high up
in the snow-capped Taurus Mountains.

Many workmen died cutting this 80-mile pass
through the Taurus mountain range.
The "Cilician Gates," shown here,
are near Tarsus and were often used by Paul.
Cyrus marched 10,000 troops through them.
Later, the Romans built a real gate across it,
maintaining a tight security over the pass.

Archaeologists date these dwellings in Tarsus
back to 2000 B.C.

ANTIOCH

Antioch in Syria,
to which Barnabas was sent,
was one of 16 cities in the ancient world
that bore that name—
all built by Syria's Seleucus I.
Josephus, the ancient Jewish historian,
says Syrian Antioch
ranked next to Rome and Alexandria
as the greatest city of its time.

Situated on the Orontes River,
Antioch was about 15 miles from Seleucia,
a seaport on the Mediterranean.
Breezes blew inland from the Mediterranean,
giving Antioch a delightful climate.
Antioch's size and nearness to the sea
made it popular with travelers and sailors.
An ancient writer says
you could sit in the public square in Antioch
and, literally, watch the world go by.

Antioch's popularity brought it problems.
At one point in history,
the city became so wild and immoral
that a Roman general made it "off limits"
to troops under his command.
It was to this kind of city that Barnabas went
to preach the Good News of Jesus.

Jesus' followers, like Jesus himself,
were especially sensitive to society's sick.
"People who are well do not need a doctor,"
Jesus said (Mark 2:17).
The early church followed Jesus' thought.

ENTER SAUL

Upon arrival at Antioch,
Barnabas saw the opportunities it offered.
Immediately he thought of Saul in Tarsus.

Barnabas went to Tarsus to look for Saul.
When he found him, he took him to Antioch,
and for a whole year
the two met with the people of the church
and taught a large group.
It was at Antioch
that the believers were first called Christians.
ACTS 11:25-26

Acts once more picks up the thread of Paul's life.
The only other source of information
about this period in Paul's career
is his own Letter to the Galatians.
There he traces his travels
from his conversion to Barnabas's arrival.

I went at once to Arabia,
and then I returned to Damascus.
It was three years later that I went to
Jerusalem. . . .
Afterward I went to places in Syria and Cilicia.
GALATIANS 1:17-21

Paul probably spent most of his time
in his hometown of Tarsus in Cilicia.
Possibly, much of this time was given
to Paul's spiritual and theological growth.
Possibly, too,
Paul did a certain amount of preaching.
If so, some of the trials and sufferings
listed in 2 Corinthians 11:23-27
could be fitted into this period of his life.

In any event,
Paul's arrival in Antioch was a milestone,
not only in his own life
but also in the life of the early church.

THE PROPHECY

In the course of the year, an event occurred
to show the spirit of early Christianity.

It was triggered by Agabus,
a man who had received the gift of prophecy.
In the formative years of the church,
this gift was not unusual (1 Corinthians 12:28).

*About that time
some prophets went from Jerusalem to Antioch.
One of them, named Agabus,
stood up and by the power of the Spirit
predicted that a severe famine
was about to come over all the earth.
(It came when Claudius was emperor.)
The disciples decided that each of them
would send as much as he could
to help their fellow believers
who lived in Judea.
They did this, then, and sent the money
to the church elders by Barnabas and Saul.*

ACTS 11:27–30

12
Great
Escape

The Master's Men
WILLIAM BARCLAY

Tacitus's *Annals* and Suetonius's *Claudius*
both mention a famine during the reign
of Claudius (A.D. 41-54),
while Josephus mentions in his *Antiquities*
that a famine peaked in Judea around A.D. 46.

The significant point, however,
is not the date of the famine
but the response of the Christians to it.

The episode ends with Saul and Barnabas
departing for Jerusalem.
They carried with them money for the poor
to help them meet the soaring cost of food.
This "famine visit" marks Paul's second visit
to Jerusalem since his conversion (Acts 9:26)
The date was about A.D. 46.

*There is a Roman coin
which has as its inscription the picture
of an ox facing an altar and a plough
with the words "Ready for either."
The ox must be ready
for the dramatic sacrifice of the altar
or the long routine of the plough.*

The ox's fate
is a dramatic illustration of the option
that lay open to many early Christians.
They might die swiftly by the sword,
or they might endure a long life of struggle.

One who died swiftly by the sword
was James, the brother of John.
James, along with Peter and John,
enjoyed a special relationship with Jesus.
The three were the only ones with Jesus
when he raised Jairus's daughter (Luke 8:51),
when he was transfigured (Luke 9:28),
and when he prayed in the garden (Mark 14:33).

Lord, Are You There?

Some years ago,
the book *The Song of Bernadette*
was topping sales in the nation's bookstores.
Then it became a movie.
The movie was prefaced by these words:

For those who believe in God,
no explanation is needed.
For those who do not believe in God,
no explanation is possible.

But what interests us here
is not *The Song of Bernadette* itself,
but the story of how it came to be written.
It goes back to World War II,
when a famous Jewish writer,
Franz Werfel,
slipped through the Nazi frontier with his wife.
The Nazis learned of their escape
and set out after them in hot pursuit.

Werfel's plan was to get to Spain
and from there
to get passage to the United States.
When he reached the Spanish border, however,
he was refused entry.

Crushed and frightened,
Werfel and his wife
took temporary refuge in a nearby village.
It happened to be Lourdes,
home of the famous shrine to Mary,
the mother of Jesus.
For decades, pilgrims from all over the world
had come to this shrine
for help and healing.

That night Werfel, too, visited the shrine.
Standing alone in the darkness,
he spoke words to this effect:

"I am not a believer,
and I must be honest and say so.

Acts reports James's death only in passing,
as it sets the stage
for Peter's arrest and escape from prison.

About this time King Herod began to persecute
some members of the church.
He had James, the brother of John, put to death
by the sword.
When he saw that this pleased the Jews,
he went ahead and had Peter arrested.

ACTS 12:1–3

HEROD AGRIPPA

The Herod here is not Herod Antipas,
Herod the Great's son, but Herod Agrippa I,
a grandson of Herod the Great.
Herod the Great ruled at Jesus' birth
(Matthew 2:1) and had a number of wives.
Herod Antipas ruled in Jesus' adulthood
(Luke 23:7).

Raised in Rome, Herod Agrippa
was a close friend of the emperor Caligula,
who gave to Agrippa the title of "king."

But in my extreme need,
on the chance that I could be wrong about God,
I ask him for help for me and my wife."

Werfel returned to the village.
Never before, he confided to a friend later,
did he experience such peace of mind
as he did after making that prayer.

Within days,
Werfel and his wife gained admittance into Spain.
Shortly after, they obtained passage
to the United States.

The first thing Werfel did
upon his safe arrival in the United States
was to write the story of Lourdes,
calling it *The Song of Bernadette.*

Many linked Werfel's prayer
to his dramatic escape from the Nazis, just as Acts
linked the Christian community's prayer
to Peter's dramatic escape from jail.

For those who do not believe in prayer,
no explanation is possible;
for those who believe in prayer, none is needed.

Some of the many crutches left at Lourdes
by people healed there.

The ancient Jewish historian Josephus
reports Agrippa died in A.D. 44.
Acts says he died suddenly and strangely.

On a chosen day Herod put on his royal robes,
sat on his throne,
and made a speech to the people.
"It isn't a man speaking, but a god!" they shouted.
At once the angel of the Lord struck Herod
down, because he did not give honor to God.
He was eaten by worms and died.

ACTS 12:21-23

Josephus reports that Herod's royal robes
were spun of silver and glittered in the sun.
The crowd's flattery was not uncommon;
Orientals frequently deified their kings.
Acts suggests Herod's sin was that he kept
the honor that belonged to God.

Josephus adds to the mystery of Herod's death,
saying that the superstitious Herod
believed an owl would trumpet his demise.
While basking in the applause of the crowd,
he spotted an owl perched on an awning.

He immediately got stomach cramps
and died within days of a "loathsome" disease.

PETER'S ESCAPE

Herod's persecution of Christians
seems to have been no more than a purge
of its leaders.
In the process, Peter was seized, tried, and jailed.

Peter was sleeping between two guards.
He was tied with two chains,
and there were guards on duty
at the prison gate.
Suddenly an angel of the Lord stood there,
and a light shone in the cell. . . .
At once the chains fell off Peter's hands. . . .
They passed by the first guard station
and then the second . . .
and suddenly the angel left Peter.

ACTS 12:6-10

Peter's dramatic escape is prefaced
by the words "the people of the church
were praying earnestly to God for him"
(Acts 12:5).

Reference to the "light" suggests, also,
something more than human instrumentality.

AFTERMATH

Peter, obviously stunned and exhilarated,
found himself standing outside the prison.

Aware of his situation,
he went to the home of Mary,
the mother of John Mark,
where many people had gathered
and were praying.
Peter knocked at the outside door,
and a servant girl named Rhoda
came to answer it.

She recognized Peter's voice and was so happy
that she ran back in without opening the door,
and announced that Peter was standing outside.
"You are crazy!" they told her.
But she insisted that it was true.
So they answered, "It is his angel."

Meanwhile Peter kept on knocking.
At last they opened the door.

ACTS 12:12-16

Some suggest that the John Mark mentioned
here is Mark the evangelist (Acts 13:5; 15:39).
Some suggest, also, that this is the same house
of the Last Supper (Luke 22:10).
It is also the site of Pentecost (Acts 1:13).

The delightful scene of Peter waiting at the door,
while Rhoda runs in circles,
is welcome humor in a stress-filled situation.
When the door was finally unbolted,
a breathless Peter stood before them.
Words and time were precious.

He motioned
with his hand for them to be quiet,
and he explained to them
how the Lord had brought him out of prison.
"Tell this to James
and the rest of the believers," he said;
then he left and went somewhere else.

ACTS 12:17

Two important points stand out.

The first is Peter's final instructions:
"Tell this to James."
This is James, "the Lord's brother"
(Galatians 1:19).
Brother, here, could mean
a blood brother or merely a kinsman.

68

This James is to be distinguished, also,
from James, the brother of John,
and James, son of Alphaeus (Luke 6:14-15).
We will meet him again during deliberations
on the status of Gentile converts in Acts 15,
and when Paul reports to him in Acts 21.
Paul mentions him in two of his letters:
1 Corinthians 15:7 and Galatians 1:19; 2:9.
Finally, authorship of the Letter from James
is attributed to him.

The significant point is this:
We meet for the first time in Acts the man
who, from this point on, succeeds Peter
as the leader of the church in Jerusalem.

The second point of interest is
the final statement about Peter:
"He left and went somewhere else."

With these words,
Peter in effect drops out of Acts.
Presumably, the price on his head
and the danger his presence created
for the Christian community were too great.
A fourth-century church historian, Eusebius,
says he eventually fled to Rome,
where he was martyred about 20 years later.

TRAGIC POSTSCRIPT

The story of Peter's dramatic escape from jail
ends with this short statement:

When morning came,
there was a tremendous confusion
among the guards—
what had happened to Peter?
Herod gave orders to search for him,
but they could not find him.
So he had the guards questioned
and ordered them put to death.

ACTS 12:18–19

These guards suffered a fate
that was not uncommon in the ancient world:
those responsible for a prisoner's escape
received the prisoner's punishment.

EPILOGUE

Luke ends his report
of the eventful happenings in Jerusalem
by returning attention to Saul and Barnabas.

Peter's dramatic escape, Herod's death,
the execution of the guards—
these events have made us forget entirely
that Saul and Barnabas had come to Jerusalem.
The importance of their visit was eclipsed,
but their mission was achieved.
Luke says simply:

Barnabas and Saul finished their mission
and returned from Jerusalem,
taking John Mark with them.

ACTS 12:25

69

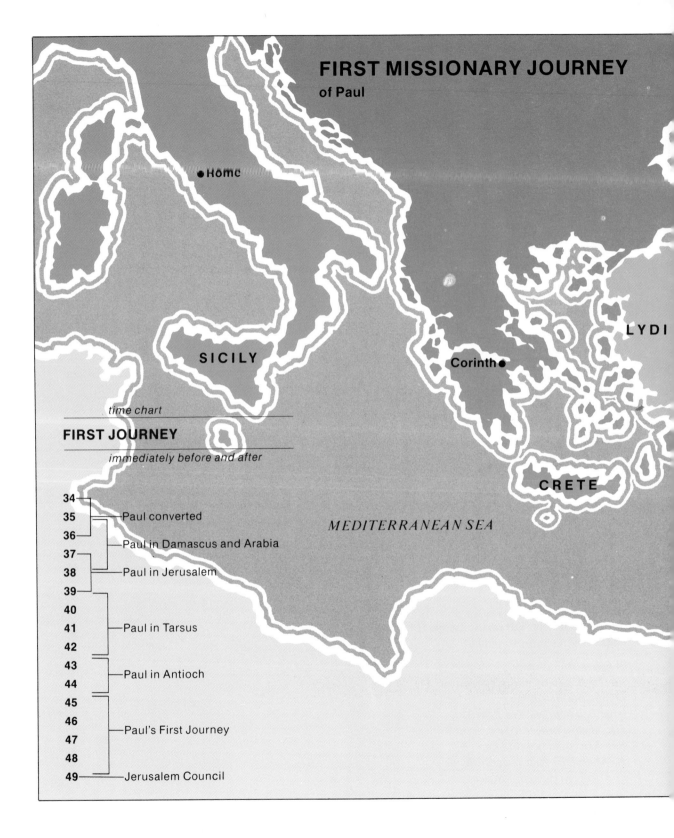

FIRST MISSIONARY JOURNEY
of Paul

●Rome

SICILY

MEDITERRANEAN SEA

Corinth●

LYDI

CRETE

time chart

FIRST JOURNEY

immediately before and after

34
35 ——Paul converted
36 ——Paul in Damascus and Arabia
37
38 ——Paul in Jerusalem
39
40
41 ——Paul in Tarsus
42
43 ——Paul in Antioch
44
45
46 ——Paul's First Journey
47
48
49——Jerusalem Council

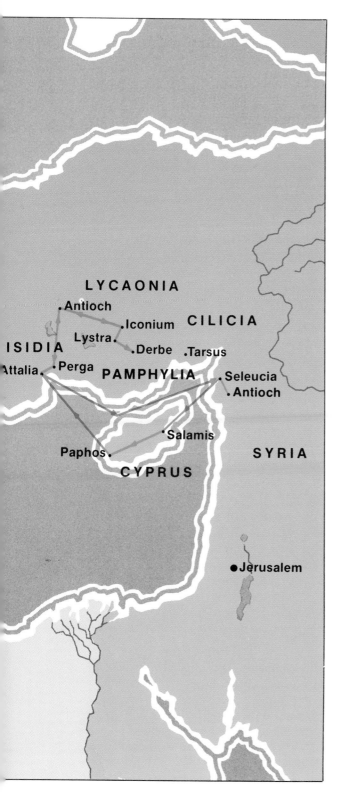

LYCAONIA

.Antioch

.Iconium CILICIA

Lystra.

ISIDIA   .Derbe   .Tarsus

Attalia. .Perga PAMPHYLIA   .Seleucia

                          .Antioch

              .Salamis

      SYRIA

Paphos.

CYPRUS

●Jerusalem

PART THREE

FIRST MISSIONARY JOURNEY

Acts 13-15

13 Great Beginning

Every movement in history has its champion.
Organized labor had Samuel Gompers.
Women's suffrage had Susan B. Anthony.
Civil rights had Martin Luther King.
Ecumenism had Pope John XXIII.
Christianity had Paul of Tarsus.

PAUL

Paul was catapulted into prominence
not by something he did
but through the power of the Holy Spirit.

In the church at Antioch
there were some prophets and teachers. . . .
While they were serving the Lord and fasting,
the Holy Spirit said to them,
"Set apart for me Barnabas and Saul,
to do the work to which I have called them."

They fasted and prayed, placed their hands
on them, and sent them off.

ACTS 13:1–3

From this point on, the Acts of the Apostles
could be called the Acts of Paul.
He dominates the church's missionary action
like the sun dominates the summer.

From this point on, also,
Paul drops the use of his Jewish name, Saul,
and uses its Roman or Gentile form, Paul—
possibly as a sign of his calling
to preach the Good News to the Gentiles.

STARTING POINT

Perhaps because Barnabas was a Cypriot,
the first port of call for the missionaries
was the island of Cyprus.

Taking young John Mark with them,
Paul and Barnabas left Antioch
for the seaport of Seleucia, 20 miles away.
There were no passenger ships in their day,
so they traveled on a cargo ship.
Fifty choppy miles later,
the cargo ship dropped anchor in Salamis Bay.

For the Christians who had fled to Cyprus
to escape persecution (Acts 11:19),
the arrival of the missionaries at Salamis
must have been big news.
Acts, however, sums up the whole visit
in one cryptic sentence:

When they arrived at Salamis,
they preached the word of God in the synagogues.

ACTS 13:5

After completing the round of synagogues,
the preachers headed overland to Paphos.
In Paul's day,
Paphos was the famous religious center
of the cult of Aphrodite, the goddess of love.
Legend says she emerged from the sea
off the coast of Cyprus.
Her reputation for prophecy was widespread.

Copper derives its name, ultimately,
from *Cyprus*.
Famous for its copper in ancient times,
Cyprus is the third largest island in the
Mediterranean, measuring 60 by 150 miles.
These ruins at Salamis are all that remain
of an old Roman gymnasium.

Tacitus reports
that the great Roman general Titus
consulted her before embarking on
his war against the Jews,
which ended in the fall of Jerusalem in A.D. 70.

When Paul and his companions
arrived in the famous religious center,
they received an invitation to preach before
"the governor of the island, Sergius Paulus"
(Acts 13:7).

Sir William Ramsay notes
that in the original Greek, Luke applies
the correct title, "proconsul," to Sergius.
He also notes a provocative archaeological find.

St. Paul the Traveller
and the Roman Citizen
WILLIAM M. RAMSAY

A Greek inscription of Soloi
on the north coast of Cyprus is dated
"in the proconsulship of Paulus,"
who probably is the same governor.

The preaching episode before the governor
turned out to be far more exciting
than anyone anticipated.

On hand was a friend of the governor,
a magician named Elymas ("the wise one").

73

This partially rebuilt Roman theater
is located on the site of ancient Salamis.

It was not unusual in those days
for men of political power and influence
to have private astrologers.
Possibly Elymas enjoyed such a post.

Elymas tried to turn Sergius against Paul.
Paul's reaction was so electrifying
that it stunned even Barnabas and Mark.

"You son of the Devil!...
You always keep trying
to turn the Lord's truth into lies!
The Lord's hand will come down on you now;
you will be blind and will not see
the light of day for a time."...

When the governor saw what had happened,
he believed.

ACTS 13:10–12

MOVING ON

From Paphos, the missionaries set sail
for Asia Minor, now modern Turkey.
Arriving on the mainland,
they went up the Kestros River to Perga.

Little is known of their stay in Perga,
but it was here—for an unknown reason—

that "John Mark left them and went back
to Jerusalem" (Acts 13:13).

After seeing John Mark off from Perga,
Paul and Barnabas
headed for the city of Pisidian Antioch
in the Galatian highlands.

Some think they headed for the highlands
because Paul suddenly became sick.
He wrote later to the Galatians:

You remember why
I preached the gospel to you the first time;
it was because I was sick.
But even though my physical condition
was a great trial to you,
you did not despise or reject me.

GALATIANS 4:13–14

What sickness Paul contracted is not known.
Some suggest it was malaria fever,
which plagued visitors to Pamphylia's lowlands.
One of the few treatments
for the burning headaches caused by malaria
was retreat to the cooler highlands.

74

Looking like a ransacked grave,
Pisidian Antioch is today
little more than a scar on the landscape.

PISIDIAN ANTIOCH

Today, the city of Pisidian Antioch
has practically disappeared
from the face of the earth.
Describing a visit to the ancient site,
a journalist writes:

"Following Paul in Turkey"
JOHN STOTT

A pair of Egyptian vultures
circled over the nearby village of Yalvac
as we drove through,
an omen of the dereliction we were to see.
For nothing is left of Pisidian Antioch
except some arches of a noble
first-century B.C. Roman aqueduct,
in a crevice of which
a pair of Black Redstarts had built their nest.

The aqueduct was used to bring water
from the mountain now called Sultan Dagh.
Archaeologists dug up terra-cotta pipes
used to carry the aqueduct water
throughout the city.

Other archaeological discoveries include
an edict designed to prevent profiteering
from grain after a severe winter
and an inscription containing the name
"Lucius Sergius Paulus the Younger"
(probably the son of the governor of Cyprus).

Upon his arrival at Pisidian Antioch,
Paul accepted an invitation
to preach in the local synagogue.
He began by reminding his listeners
how God rescued the Jews from Egypt,
made them into a powerful nation,
and gave them a great king, David.

Then Paul announced the Good News
about Jesus—"a descendant of David,
whom God made the Savior of the people
of Israel, as he had promised" (Acts 13:23).

Next, Paul explained in detail
how the religious leaders of Jerusalem
failed to recognize their Savior, pointing out:

"They made the prophets' words
come true by condemning Jesus. . . .
And after they had done everything
that the Scriptures say about him,
they took him down from the cross
and placed him in a tomb.
But God raised him from death. . . .
And we are here
to bring the Good News to you. . . .
It is through Jesus
that the message about the forgiveness of sins
is preached to you."

ACTS 13:27–32, 39

75

This broken aqueduct at Pisidian Antioch
yields the clue for the death
of so many great cities in Asia Minor.

How Did They Die?

In the Steps of St. Paul
H. V. MORTON

One barbarian with a pick-axe
can turn your city into a parched desert.
Once the aqueduct is broken,
the life of the city is ended.

The aqueduct pipe was the jugular vein
of the city of ancient Asia Minor.

When the fragile pipe was smashed,
it was just a matter of time
before gardens turned back into dust,
birds nested in the city's fountains,
and jackals roamed the city's streets.

The Turkish conquest of Asia Minor
turned the exciting cities of Paul's time
into crumbling rubble.

When the congregation heard this,
they were excited,
especially the Gentile converts to Judaism.

The next Sabbath
nearly everyone in the town came
to hear the word of the Lord.
When the Jews saw the crowds,
they were filled with jealousy;
they disputed what Paul was saying. . . .
But Paul and Barnabas
spoke out even more boldly:

"It was necessary that the word of God
should be spoken first to you.
But since you reject it . . .
we will leave you and go to the Gentiles. . . ."

When the Gentiles heard this, they were glad. . . .

But the Jews . . . started a persecution
against Paul and Barnabas
and threw them out of their region.

ACTS 13:44–50

Then the two apostles headed for Iconium.

14
Mistaken for Gods

Someone asked a famous preacher,
"What's the secret of your success?"

"It's simple," replied the preacher.
"I read myself full. I think myself clear.
I pray myself hot. And I let myself go."

Paul and Barnabas had plenty of time
to read, think, and pray
as they walked the 60 miles from Antioch
to Iconium.
And, indeed, they needed the time.
They began to see their preaching task
was going to be harder than anticipated.

Ambassador for Christ
WILLIAM BARCLAY

Yet it never even struck them to turn back.
In the Iliad, Homer tells of Achilles
being told by the prophetess
that if he goes out to a certain battle
he will be killed.
"Nevertheless," answers the Greek hero,
"I am for going on."
No matter what lay ahead,
Paul and Barnabas were for going on.

ICONIUM

The two apostles probably reached Iconium
on the second or third day of their trip.
Today, the site of ancient Iconium
has been transformed into
a modern Turkish city, Konya.
It numbers about 300,000 people
and is famous for its rug industry.

Paul's preaching in Iconium was
a replay of what happened in Antioch.
It touched off both a wave of conversion
and a riot.

Paul and Barnabas went to the synagogue
and spoke in such a way
that a great number of Jews and Gentiles
became believers.
But the Jews who would not believe
stirred up the Gentiles
and turned them against the believers.
The apostles stayed there for a long time,
speaking boldy about the Lord, who proved
that their message about his grace was true
by giving them the power
to perform miracles and wonders.
The people of the city were divided:
some were for the Jews,
others for the apostles.

ACTS 14:1-4

In time, the situation got so ugly
that Paul and Barnabas were advised
to leave the city.

As the apostles bade farewell
to the small community of Christian converts,
they took comfort in one fact:
the seed of faith had been planted.
There was nothing more they could do now
but pray that this fragile sprout
would take root. It did.

The God Hermes,
for whom the people of Lystra
mistook Paul, is shown here.
The sculptured relief
is from the bottom drum
of one of the enormous 60-foot
columns that once graced
the Temple of Artemis
in Ephesus.
Later,
when Paul preached in Ephesus,
he would have certainly admired
this relief and, possibly,
recalled the Lystra episode.

Close-up of the God Hermes

LYSTRA

After leaving Iconium,
Paul and Barnabas made their way to Lystra.
Today, little remains of that ancient city.
Archaeologists, however,
have unearthed two interesting remains.

The first is a stone slab
containing the city's name in Latin, *Lustra,*
along with evidence that the city
held the status of a Roman colony.

A Roman colony was a "miniature Rome,"
in that the Roman citizens living there
spoke Latin, dressed Roman,
and were ruled by their own Roman officials.

The second interesting remains is an altar
to Hermes and the "hearer of prayer,"
which probably refers to the god Zeus.
These two gods conditioned
a wild welcome for Paul and Barnabas
when they first preached in the city.

In Lystra there was a crippled man
who had been lame from birth
and had never been able to walk.
He sat there and listened to Paul's words.
Paul saw that he believed and could be healed,
so he looked straight at him
and said in a loud voice,
"Stand up straight on your feet!"
The man jumped up
and started walking around.
When the crowds saw what Paul had done,
they started shouting
in their own Lycaonian language,
"The gods have become like men
and have come down to us!"
They gave Barnabas the name Zeus,
and Paul the name Hermes,
because he was the chief speaker.

This camel-humped hill
houses the bricks and lintels of ancient Lystra.
Pieces of columns litter the slope,
now the playground of moles and squirrels.
Had Paul not preached at Lystra,
the city would probably no longer
be remembered.

The priest of the god Zeus,
whose temple stood just outside the town,
brought bulls and flowers to the gate,
for he and the crowds
wanted to offer sacrifice to the apostles.

ACTS 14:8–13

Why this surprising reaction?
A clue is contained in Ovid's *Metamorphoses.*
There the first-century poet describes
a legendary visit of Zeus and Hermes to Lystra.
The disguised gods got a cold welcome.

To a thousand houses did they go,
asking for lodging and for rest.
A thousand houses did the bolts fasten
against them.

Finally, the weary gods
came to a tiny hut "thatched with straw."

79

The elderly peasant occupants,
Philemon and his wife, Baucis
received them warmly and fed them.

Before departing,
the gods punished the unfriendly townspeople.
They rewarded the elderly peasants, however,
by transforming their tiny hut
into a magnificent temple.

Perhaps the townspeople
remembered this ancient legend
and didn't want to repeat the mistake.
Paul and Barnabas protested to the people:

"We ourselves are only human beings like you!
We are here to announce the Good News,
to turn you away from these worthless things
to the living God, who made heaven, earth, sea,
and all that is in them.
In the past
he allowed all people to go their own way.
But he has always given evidence
of his existence by the good things he does:
he gives you rain from heaven
and crops at the right times;
he gives you food
and fills your hearts with happiness."

ACTS 14:15-17

It was the first time
Paul attempted to preach the Good News
to a pagan audience.
Paul's style was to begin with the things
his hearers could see and touch.

Lystra was famous for its grain crops,
and the people were justly proud
of themselves, their fields, and their crops.
Paul began by explaining that God
made them, their fields, their crops,
and the rain and sun they depended on.

Paul's introduction was not unlike
that of the legendary desert nomad.
Someone asked him,
"How can you be so sure there is a God?"
The nomad replied,
"The same way
that I know a man has crossed the desert
when I look at the sand!
I see God's footprints everywhere I look."

TROUBLE AGAIN

Paul's preaching in Lystra
was cut short by the arrival
of some Jews from Antioch and Iconium.
Probably they had come to purchase grain,
but they were incensed
to find Paul still preaching in their region.

Eastern peoples, even in modern times,
have ways of dealing with unwanted outsiders.
Some years ago, for example,
a tourist was traveling in the area of Nablus.

The Life of Paul
BENJAMIN WILLARD ROBINSON

Suddenly a stone
thrown from a considerable distance
fell into the road beside him.
Before the dust of that stone
and the alarm it caused had subsided,
another one struck his horse . . .
causing the animal to rear and jump.
This was followed by many more,
mostly from unseen sources.
Fortunately he was wearing a stiff rubber helmet
so that his head was safe.
But that morning was one never to be
forgotten. . . .
Somewhat the same way it happened to Paul.

80

While the mother city, Perga, lies in ruins,
Attalia, its former port, thrives.

Paul Sailed from Here

Pirate raids were a constant menace
to the coastal cities of Asia Minor.
To guard against these blitzlike attacks,
Perga was built several miles inland.
It was linked to the port of Attalia
by the Kestros River. Acts says:

[Paul and Barnabas]
preached the message in Perga
and then went to Attalia,
and from there they sailed back to Antioch.

ACTS 14:25–26

Alexander the Great
made Perga the jumping-off point
for his invasion of inner Asia Minor.
Today, the city is a sea of rubble,
dominated by the theater in the foreground.

81

Acts says of the newly arrived Jews:

*They won the crowds over to their side,
stoned Paul
and dragged him out of the town,
thinking that he was dead.
But when the believers gathered around him,
he got up and went back into the town.
The next day he and Barnabas
went to Derbe.*

ACTS 14:19-20

15

Giant Step

DERBE

Today, the probable site of ancient Derbe
is a green mound surrounded by a swamp.

The book of Acts
reports the Derbe visit in one sentence:

*Paul and Barnabas
preached the Good News in Derbe
and won many disciples.*

ACTS 14:21

Acts concludes:

*Then they went back to Lystra,
to Iconium, and on to Antioch in Pisidia.
They strengthened the believers
and encouraged them
to remain true to the faith. . . .*

*After going through the territory of Pisidia,
they came to Pamphylia.
There they preached the message in Perga
and then went to Attalia,
and from there they sailed back to Antioch.*

ACTS 14:21-26

When Paul and Barnabas arrived home,
they were surely exhausted.
They had been on the road four long years.
The date was A.D. 49.

The film *Lili* concerns a young girl
who is a member of a traveling circus.
One day she becomes depressed,
feeling that no one loves her.
Her only friends
are four puppets in one of the sideshows.
She decides to run away.

Before leaving, however,
she goes to say good-bye to the puppets.
As the puppets hug her tightly and weep,
Lili suddenly feels them trembling.
Only then does she realize
that the puppeteer is the one who loves her.
The puppets are merely the vehicles
through which he expresses his love for her.

Lili had mistaken the gifts for the giver.
She had failed to distinguish the "packages"
from the "gift of love" inside them.

The point is this:
The "packages" are secondary;
the important thing is the "gifts" inside them.

Confusing "packages" and "gifts"
seems to have been at the heart
of another misunderstanding in Paul's time.

Many Jewish Christians
felt the old structures and rituals of Judaism
must be observed, even by Gentile Christians.
They had overlooked, apparently,
Jesus' teaching concerning the relationship
between structures and persons. Jesus said:

"The Sabbath was made for the good of man;
man was not made for the Sabbath.
So the Son of Man is Lord even of the Sabbath."

MARK 2:27–28

Jesus used the following example
to prepare his followers
for the new rituals and structures
that would have to accompany his teaching.

"No one patches up an old coat
with a piece of new cloth,
for the new patch will shrink
and make an even bigger hole in the coat.
Nor does anyone pour new wine
into used wineskins, for the skins will burst,
the wine will pour out,
and the skins will be ruined.
Instead, new wine is poured into fresh
wineskins, and both will keep
in good condition."

MATTHEW 9:16–17

The question of imposing
traditional Jewish rituals and practices
on new Gentile Christians had arisen earlier
in the case of Cornelius.
An exception was made in his case,
but the rule remained.
Now the same question reasserted itself:
Must Gentiles, unfamiliar with Judaism,
become Jews before becoming Christians?
Acts describes the dilemma:

Some men came from Judea to Antioch
and started teaching the believers,

"You cannot be saved
unless you are circumcised
as the Law of Moses requires."
Paul and Barnabas
got into a fierce argument with them about this,
so it was decided that Paul and Barnabas
and some of the others in Antioch
should go to Jerusalem
and see the apostles and elders about this.

ACTS 15:1–2

Paul and Barnabas, once again,
made the long journey back to Jerusalem.

THE DISCUSSION

After a long debate
Peter stood up and said,
"My brothers, you know that a long time ago
God chose me from among you
to preach the Good News to the Gentiles,
so that they could hear and believe.
And God . . .
showed his approval of the Gentiles
by giving the Holy Spirit to them. . . .
He made no difference between us and them. . . .
We believe and are saved by the grace
of the Lord Jesus, just as they are."

ACTS 15:7–11

Peter makes this important point:
We are saved by the grace of Jesus,
not by the Law.
For Paul, the Law was a temporary guide
whose purpose
was to prepare the way for Jesus.
Now that the "gift" is in our midst,
the "package" is no longer needed.

In other words,
the Law has served its purpose well.
It is no longer needed.

Norias, or "bucket" waterwheels like this,
turned and splashed on the Orontes River
in Paul's day.
The river was largely unnavigable,
but its valley formed a major trade highway
between Palestine and Asia Minor.
Paul and Barnabas undoubtedly used it.
This noria is near Hamah in modern Syria.

This fact, along with his role
in the first council in the church's history,
gave added weight to his words.
They sealed the decision.

Then the apostles and the elders,
together with the whole church,
decided to choose some men from the group
and send them to Antioch
with Paul and Barnabas. They chose . . .
Judas, called Barsabbas, and Silas,
and they sent the following letter by them:

"We, the apostles and the elders,
your brothers, send greetings
to all our brothers of Gentile birth
who live in Antioch, Syria, and Cilicia. . . .

"The Holy Spirit and we have agreed
not to put any other burden on you
besides these necessary rules:
eat no food that has been offered to idols;
eat no blood;
eat no animal that has been strangled;
and keep yourselves from sexual immorality." . . .

When the people read it,
they were filled with joy by the message.

ACTS 15:22–31

Then James spoke up:

"Listen to me, my brothers!
Simon has just explained how God
first showed his care for the Gentiles. . . .
The words of the prophets
agree completely with this.
As the scripture says,
'After this I will return, says the Lord. . . .
All the rest of mankind will come to me,
all the Gentiles whom I have called. . . .'

"It is my opinion . . .
that we should not trouble the Gentiles
who are turning to God."

ACTS 15:13–19

THE DECISION

James's support of Peter was important,
because James was a conscientious observer
of the Mosaic Law.
Even the strictest rabbi would not
have found fault with James's observance.

The introductory formula
"The Holy Spirit and we have agreed"
expresses faith in the Holy Spirit's presence
in the council's deliberation.

The ossuaries
in this burial cave on the Mount of Olives
date from the first century.

Whose Bones?

Diggers unearthed several ossuaries,
or stone burial chambers of human bones,
outside Jerusalem in 1945.

A coin of Agrippa I and pottery remnants
suggest the burial site
dates from the first century A.D.

One ossuary bore crosslike marks.
Another bore a blurred Greek inscription,
which one scholar translated "Jesus help"—
possibly a Christian prayer.
A third bore the name "Simeon Barsaba."

Three questions arise.
Are the crosslike marks Christian symbols
or Jewish marks like those in Ezekiel 9:4?
Is the blurred inscription a Christian prayer?
Is Simeon Barsaba a Christian, related
to Judas Barsabbas (Aramaic: bar sa'ba)
who, with Silas, carried the church's letter
to Gentile Christians (Acts 15:22-23)?

Like so many intriguing possibilities,
these three questions hang in the air
awaiting the verdict of time and research.

This same faith continues to this day,
when representatives of the church
meet together in council
on a church-wide level.

The four prescriptions set down for Gentiles
are clearly unequal in weight and importance.
The first three seem to be
a practical compromise on nonessentials.
Refraining from food offered to idols,
for example, avoided the impression
of participation in false worship.
The nonessential nature of this prescription
seems clear from 1 Corinthians 8:1-13.

The fourth prescription, on the other hand,
is one that Paul refers to again and again
on many occasions (1 Corinthians 5:15-20).

The all-important decision of the council,
however, is that Gentiles are saved
by the "grace of the Lord Jesus"
and not by conformity to external practices
and observances of Judaism.

When the council ended,
Paul and Barnabas returned to Antioch.
The church had taken a great step forward
in reaching out to all peoples of all nations.

PART FOUR

SECOND MISSIONARY JOURNEY
of Paul

Rome

MACEDONIA

SAMOTHRACE

Philippi.

Neapolis

Thessalonica.

Berea.

Troas

SICILY

Corinth

Athens

Ephesus

CRETE

MEDITERRANEAN SEA

time chart

SECOND JOURNEY

immediately before and during

49 ——— Jerusalem Council

50

—— Paul's Second Journey

51

– – – 1–2 Thessalonians

52

SECOND MISSIONARY JOURNEY

Acts 16-18

16
The Vision

Never in history have so many soldiers
returned to so many battlefields
as the soldiers of World War II.
They return to Europe and to the Pacific
to rendezvous with the past.

"Back to Bataan"
CHARLES N. BARNARD

Like ocean salmon
returning to the streams of their birth,
old soldiers may not understand
the reasons for their pilgrimages;
yet they make them. . . .

One man
had come back to Corregidor four times. Why?
"Because this is where
the most exciting events of my life took place.
I never did anything later in life to equal it."

Like these soldiers,
Paul felt the desire to return to the towns
where, almost five years earlier,
he had preached the Good News of Jesus.

Paul said to Barnabas,
"Let us go back and visit our brothers
in every town
where we preached the word of the Lord,
and let us find out
how they are getting along."

ACTS 15:36

Barnabas liked the idea
and wanted to take John Mark with them.
But Paul was against this
because Mark had not stayed with them
the first time they visited these towns..

There was a sharp argument,
and they separated:
Barnabas took Mark and sailed off for Cyprus,
while Paul chose Silas.

ACTS 15:39–40

Later, Paul would have a change of heart
about Mark (2 Timothy 4:11).
For the present, however, they separated.

TIMOTHY

Paul traveled on to Derbe and Lystra,
where a Christian named Timothy lived.
His mother, who was also a Christian,
was Jewish, but his father was a Greek.
All the believers in Lystra and Iconium
spoke well of Timothy.

ACTS 16:1–2

When Paul met the young man,
he was delighted and invited him
to go along with Silas and himself
as they visited with the Christian groups
in the area.

As they went through the towns,
they delivered to the believers
the rules decided upon
by the apostles and elders in Jerusalem,
and they told them to obey those rules.
So the churches were made stronger
in the faith and grew in numbers every day.

ACTS 16:4–5

At the trip's end,
Paul's admiration for Timothy was great.

The seaport city of Neapolis
(modern Kavalla), shown here,
prizes an ancient Roman aqueduct
that was used right into modern times
to channel water down from Mount Pangeus.

Jumping-off Point

The ferocious sea god, Poseidon,
is portrayed in Homer's *Iliad*
as sitting on a mountain crag of Samothrace
watching two armies clash on the mainland.

Samothrace is a small, mountainous island.
One of its peaks
soars well over 5,000 feet into the air.
Paul caught a good wind
to make the island in a day (Acts 16:11).

After spending the night on Samothrace,
the two missionaries crossed over to Neapolis,
the seaport for Philippi, some miles inland.

In the years ahead,
Timothy would become Paul's close co-worker
and the recipient of two of his letters.

TO EUROPE

Paul's next stop was the city of Troas,
which was near the walled city of Troy.
Legend says Greek soldiers captured Troy
by hiding inside a massive wooden horse.
Unsuspecting citizens found the odd object
and pulled it inside their fortified city.

While at Troas, Paul had a vision
of "a Macedonian standing and begging him,
'Come over to Macedonia and help us'"
(Acts 16:9).

The report of the vision is followed by
the first of the four "we" sections in Acts
(16:10-17; 20:5-16; 21:1-18; 27:1-28:16).

"We" is regarded as a possible indication
that Luke was with Paul
as an eyewitness companion at this point.

The coincidence of Paul's Macedonian vision
with the first "we" section
has sparked a variety of speculations.
Was Luke the "Macedonian" in the vision?
Did Luke, a doctor (Colossians 4:14),
join Paul now because he needed medical care,
stemming from his illness (Galatians 4:13)?
We cannot be certain.

What is certain, however,
is that Paul's vision marked a turning point
in his missionary activity.
He now headed for Europe proper.

As Paul sailed from Troas
toward Neapolis on the coast of Europe,
a meditation may have suggested itself.

The Acts of the Apostles
WILLIAM BARCLAY

The full name of Troas
was Alexandrian Troas after Alexander.
Just across the sea was Philippi,
called after Alexander's father.
Farther on was Thessalonica
called after Alexander's half-sister.
The district was permeated with memories
of Alexander;
and Alexander was the man who had said
that his aim was "to marry the east to the west"
and so make one world.

If Alexander's primary aim had been
the "political marriage" of east and west,
Paul's primary aim was now
the "spiritual marriage" of east and west.

Reflecting on the importance
of Paul's crossing into Europe,
a modern British TV celebrity mused:

Paul: Envoy Extraordinary
MALCOLM MUGGERIDGE AND ALEC VIDLER

I don't suppose that he had much baggage
with him, but he was carrying a great light
to shine in the darkness of a sick world. . . .

It is difficult also
to think of any comparable arrival.
Perhaps, on an infinitely lower scale,
Lenin arriving unknown at the Finland Station
in Petrograd in 1917.
At the time nobody could have guessed
what would come of that.
Paul's arrival touched off two thousand years
of history, the story of Christendom.

PHILIPPI

After Paul landed at Neapolis,
he began the trip inland,
along the Via Egnatia, to Philippi.

Philippi was a thriving city in Paul's time.
It was also the site
where Octavian, Julius Caesar's adopted son,
defeated his father's assassins.
When Octavian became Rome's first emperor,
he remembered Philippi warmly,
conferring on it the status of a Roman colony.
Possibly, Paul and Luke talked about this
as they entered the city.

Luke describes their first efforts
to preach the Good News to the Philippians.

On the Sabbath
we went out of the city to the riverside,
where we thought there would be a place
where Jews gathered for prayer.
We sat down and talked to the women
who gathered there.

ACTS 16:13

Today, Philippi is a ghost town.
These broken columns identify the location
of the square into which Paul and Silas
were dragged and beaten (Acts 16:23).

At the foot of this mountain fortification
once lay Philippi's city square (left)
and amphitheater (right).

Archaeologists unearthed an arched gateway
on the western side of Philippi.
Under it passed the Egnatian Way;
and, about a mile outside the city,
the roadway passed over a small river.
Scholars identify this spot as the "riverside"
where the "Jews gathered for prayer,"
possibly because the group was so small
that it didn't need a synagogue.

Indeed, the "riverside" meeting place
may have even been inspired by Psalm 137.

It describes Jews, far away from home,
meeting in a similar setting centuries before.

By the rivers of Babylon we sat down;
there we wept when we remembered Zion.
On the willows near by we hung up our harps.
Those who captured us told us to sing;
they told us to entertain them:
"Sing us a song about Zion."

PSALM 137:1–3

The riverside beginning
of Paul's preaching in the western world
suggests another association.

It was by a riverside in the eastern world
that Jesus was baptized
to begin his own preaching of the Good News.
And it was by a riverside, too,
that Jesus chose two of his first disciples
(John 1:35).

Paul's riverside mission effort ended,
as it did for Jesus in the east,
with baptism and discipleship.
One of the new Christians
opened her home to Paul and Luke,
anticipating Peter's exhortation
to later Christians.

Love one another earnestly. . . .
Open your homes to each other.

1 PETER 4:8-9

The Via Egnatia, now returning to dust,
once echoed to the sound of Paul's footsteps.

Paul Traveled This Road

Looking like a great stone snake,
this ancient Roman road
is part of a web of 50,000 miles of roads
that linked 43 Roman provinces around A.D. 200.

Most roads had shoulders.
They were excavated down to bedrock
and surfaced with carefully fitted stones.
Many are still in use today.

Along this famous Via Egnatia—
linking Neapolis, Philippi, and Thessalonica—
generals cantered home after great battles,
eastern traders carted spices to big cities,
and poor vagabonds trudged barefoot.

All are forgotten now.
Only one traveler from ancient times
is remembered—Paul.
For it was along this very road
that he walked inland to set up
the first Christian church on European soil.

THE SLAVE GIRL

But a painful ordeal lay ahead of them.
Luke writes:

One day
as we were going to the place of prayer,
we were met by a slave girl
who had an evil spirit
that enabled her to predict the future.
She earned a lot of money for her owners
by telling fortunes.

ACTS 16.16

Persons of this kind
were not uncommon in ancient times.

The Acts of the Apostles
WILLIAM BARCLAY

She was what was called a Pytho,
that is, a person who could give oracles
to guide men about the future.
She was mad and the ancient world
had a strange respect for mad people,
because, they said, the gods had taken away
their wits in order to put the mind of gods
into them.

When Paul exorcised the evil spirit
from the possessed slave girl,
her owners flew into a rage.

They seized Paul and Silas
and dragged them to the authorities. . . .
"These men are Jews,
and they are causing trouble in our city.
They are teaching customs
that are against our law;
we are Roman citizens,
and we cannot accept these customs
or practice them."
And the crowd joined in the attack.

ACTS 16:19-22

The authorities punished the foreigners
and ordered them confined to jail.
That night, however, a violent earthquake
rocked the city, severely damaging the jail.

The jailer woke up,
and when he saw the prison doors open,
he thought that the prisoners had escaped;
so he pulled out his sword
and was about to kill himself.
But Paul shouted at the top of his voice,
"Don't harm yourself! We are all here!"

The jailer called for a light, rushed in,
and fell trembling at the feet of Paul and Silas.
Then he led them out and asked,
"Sirs, what must I do to be saved?"

They answered, "Believe in the Lord Jesus,
and you will be saved—you and your family."
Then they preached the word of the Lord
to him and to all the others in the house . . .
and he and all his family were baptized. . . .

The next morning the Roman authorities
sent police officers with the orders,
"Let those men go." . . .

Paul and Silas left the prison
and went to Lydia's house.
There they met the believers,
spoke words of encouragement to them, and left.

ACTS 16:27-35, 40

Inscribed in Greek,
this slab lists the names
of six politarchs.
Two of the names,
dating from the rule
of Emperor Claudius
(A.D. 41-54), coincide with
the time of Paul's visit
to Thessalonica.

Luke's Accuracy

"He must be confused on this point!
There's no evidence in history
indicating that officials bearing this title
ever ruled in Thessalonica."

That's what some scholars
said about Luke's reference to politarchs
("city authorities") in Acts 17:9.

Then archaeologists
uncovered a six-foot white marble slab
listing the names of six officials
who governed Thessalonica under this title.

The slab,
once part of Thessalonica's Vardar Gate,
joins a growing body of evidence
testifying to Luke's care and accuracy
in documenting his narratives in Acts.

17

Storms and Calms

Jewish Zealots (freedom fighters)
were kicking up a storm,
not only in their homeland of Judea,
but also in Roman-ruled cities outside Judea.
Even Rome did not escape their activity.

In fact, the storm in Rome became so critical
that the Roman emperor, Claudius,
expelled all Jews from the city—
and Christians with them (Acts 18:2).

This helps to explain
the furor that exploded in Thessalonica
shortly after Paul began to preach there.
A seaport city,
Thessalonica lay 90 miles from Philippi
on the Via Egnatia.

When Macedonia became a Roman province,
Thessalonica became its capital.
The city had a Jewish population
large enough to support a major synagogue.

According to his usual habit
Paul went to the synagogue.
There during three Sabbaths
he held discussions with the people,
quoting and explaining the Scriptures,
and proving from them that the Messiah
had to suffer and rise from death.
"This Jesus whom I announce to you,"
Paul said, "is the Messiah."

ACTS 17:2-3

TROUBLE

Paul's words moved many of his hearers.
Some Jews, however, opposed Paul violently.
They went so far as to arrange a raid
on the house of a man named Jason,
with whom Paul and Silas were staying.

But when they did not find them,
they dragged Jason and some other believers
before the city authorities and shouted,
"These men have caused trouble everywhere!
Now they have come to our city,
and Jason has kept them in his house.
They are all breaking the laws of the Emperor,
saying that there is another king,
whose name is Jesus."

ACTS 17:6-7

When the politarchs heard the charges,
they did not take them lightly.
Nor did they take lightly the reports
that Paul was talking about
a "future coming of Jesus" (1 Thessalonians 1:10).
This was prediction, something Rome forbade.

Prediction was an exercise of which
one emperor after another disapproved:
prediction
could too easily be used as a political weapon.
Augustus, in A.D. 11,
had issued a decree forbidding it;
this decree was reinforced on pain of death
by Tiberius in A.D. 16.

Would-be revolutionaries used prediction
to sway the gullible masses.
Paul's "prediction" was doubly dangerous
because it involved the coming of someone
who might be, indeed, a rival of the emperor.

Paul's new converts in Thessalonica
feared for his continued safety.

As soon as night came,
the believers sent Paul and Silas to Berea.

ACTS 17:10

Berea (modern Verria) was off the beaten path.
Cicero called it an "out-of-the-way town."
It would be a safe place for Paul to stay
until the Thessalonian situation cooled down.

BEREA

Paul immediately began to preach the word
in Berea.
The response to his message was positive.

They listened to the message
with great eagerness,
and every day they studied the Scriptures
to see if what Paul said was really true.
Many of them believed.

ACTS 17:11-12

The seed of faith planted by Paul
in Berea grew mightily, as this journalist notes.

Archaeologists found this dedication stone
while excavating an ancient amphitheater
near Caesarea-on-the-Sea in June 1961.
It is part of a dedication to Tiberius Caesar
by Pontius Pilate, Prefect of Judea.

The first line reads TIBERIEUM;
the second, [PON] TIUS PILATUS;
the third, [PRAEF] ECTUS IUDA [EAE].

The Wounded Fox

No one knew why
Emperor Tiberius allowed Pilate to rule Judea
for ten long years, from A.D. 27 to 36.
Pilate's high-handedness did much
to cause his Jewish subjects to hate Rome.

Stewart Perowne says that when Tiberius
was eventually pressed to explain his action,
he responded by telling an Aesop fable.

A hedgehog came upon a wounded fox.
When the hog began to brush away flies
feeding on the fox's cuts and bruises,
the fox scolded,
"Leave them be; they are already half full.
If you chase them away,
you only make room for hungrier newcomers."

The Journeys of St. Paul
STEWART PEROWNE

*The truth was that Tiberius, now seventy-seven,
after a bitter and frustrated life,
had practically abdicated. . . .
No wonder the administration of the empire
had suffered, and nowhere more
than in the highly sensitive province of Judea
which, because of its geographical position
between Egypt and Syria
and its proximity to Parthia,
was of first importance to Rome.*

*I motored out to Verria one morning
with a young man. . . .
He was anxious to show me
a number of "hidden" churches in Verria
which, he assured me,
I should never discover by myself. . . .*

*[Upon our arrival in Verria,
we were met by an elderly woman.]
She led the way down the wooden stairs
towards a stone building. . . .
It looked like a small barn. . . .
When we entered, we discovered
that the outer walls were camouflage.
They had been built
to conceal the building within them,
a diminutive Byzantine church,
probably of the fourteenth century. . . .
Dust lay thickly over everything.
Admirable frescoes covered walls and dome,
and the church
when full might have held forty persons.*

*"There are more than twenty churches
hidden away in Verria," said my acquaintance.
"They are Byzantine churches
which were concealed from the Turks."*

PERSECUTION

The Turks were not the first
to persecute the Christians in Berea.
Persecution was introduced almost immediately,
in Paul's time.

*When the Jews of Thessalonica heard
that Paul had preached the word of God
in Berea also, they came there
and started exciting and stirring up the mobs.*

At once the believers sent Paul away . . .
but both Silas and Timothy stayed in Berea.

ACTS 17:13-14

Paul set out for Athens,
leaving instructions for Silas and Timothy
to join him as soon as possible.

ATHENS

When Paul arrived in Athens,
he spent several days walking about the city,
studying it.

He was greatly upset
when he noticed how full of idols the city was.
So he held discussions in the synagogue
with the Jews
and with the Gentiles who worshiped God,
and also in the public square every day
with the people who happened to come by.
Certain Epicurean and Stoic teachers
also debated with him.

ACTS 17:16-18

EPICUREANS

Epicureans took their name from Epicurus,
whose influence spanned 300 years.
Accepting the atom theory
of the Greek philosopher Democritus,
Epicurus held that life was the result
of a chance coming together of atoms.
Death was simply their breaking up.
There was no such thing as life after death.

Epicureans philosophized
that the goal of life should be pleasure.
But they did not mean pleasure
in the sense of bodily pleasure alone.

They took a long-range picture,
holding virtue to be productive
of the greatest pleasure,
because it generated the greatest happiness
in the long run.

STOICS

Paul was familiar with Stoic thought.
His birthplace was a center of Stoic learning.
Paul's style shows traces of Stoic influence.
For example, he handled the diatribe with skill.
This conversational style of argumentation
combines brief sentence structure
with questions and objections
by a fictitious opponent.
Good illustrations of Pauline diatribe are
Romans 2:1-24 and 1 Corinthians 9.

Stoics trace their origin to a penniless Cypriot
who came to Athens in 314 B.C.
Dubbed "the Egyptian" because of his skin,
he was a philosopher and teacher.
Since he had no funds, he used the stoa,
or covered walkways, as his classrooms.
Hence his students were called Stoics.

Stoics philosophized
that life originated with a kind of fiery spirit.
A "spark" of that spirit animates everyone.
At death, it returns to its original source.

Stoics had an interesting theory
concerning the originating spirit.
They held it to be devoid of feeling,
reasoning that if it possessed feelings,
people could render it sad or glad
and thus, for the moment,
exercise limited control over it.

Stoics believed that the goal of life
was to imitate the spirit
and banish all feeling from one's life.

Whatever fate life brought,
it should be accepted gracefully.
"If you don't get what you want,
then learn to want what you get."

Stoics maintained
that even floods and famines had a purpose—
perhaps to control population.

The Letters of Paul
CALVIN J. ROETZEL

*"God" for the Stoics
was less a divine personality
who actively engaged in the affairs of men
than a divine principle (*logos *or reason)
which pervaded and governed the universe. . . .
Chrysippus once remarked
that even the lowly bedbug was an instrument
of the divine* logos *because he kept man
from sleeping too much or too long.
Once a person understood the universe
to be fundamentally rational,
he could accept whatever happened
with equanimity (or* apatheia*).
Apatheia *was not mere resignation
(as its English cognate* apathy *would suggest)
but a source of strength
based on the conviction that all things
were controlled and directed by divine reason.*

NONSENSE

It is against this background
that we must understand the problems
Stoics and Epicureans had with Paul's teaching.
"God is a loving father?
This is foolishness!" responded the Stoics.
"Life after death?
This is nonsense!" scoffed the Epicureans.

98

But Still Beautiful

"An old lady in slippers,
sitting by the fireside,
sipping barley water"—
that's how one Greek author
around Paul's time described Athens.

Yet there was still much beauty in Athens.
One sight that surely touched
the poetic soul of Paul was the acropolis.
This amazing hill of rock jutted into the air
to the height of about a 50-story building.

Paul would have shielded his eyes
from the glaring, bright Athen's sun
to study two great structures on top of it.

The first was the Parthenon,
whose white marble ruins remain to this day.

The second was a giant bronze statue
of Athena.
Pausanias, a world traveler who visited Athens
around A.D. 150,
said it towered over the landscape so high
that sailors at sea could see the setting sun
reflect off the helmet and spear of Athena.

Close-up of the Parthenon on the acropolis,
as seen from nearby Muses Hill.

In Paul's day
Athens may have looked like this.

Aerial view of the acropolis,
showing the ruins of the Parthenon.

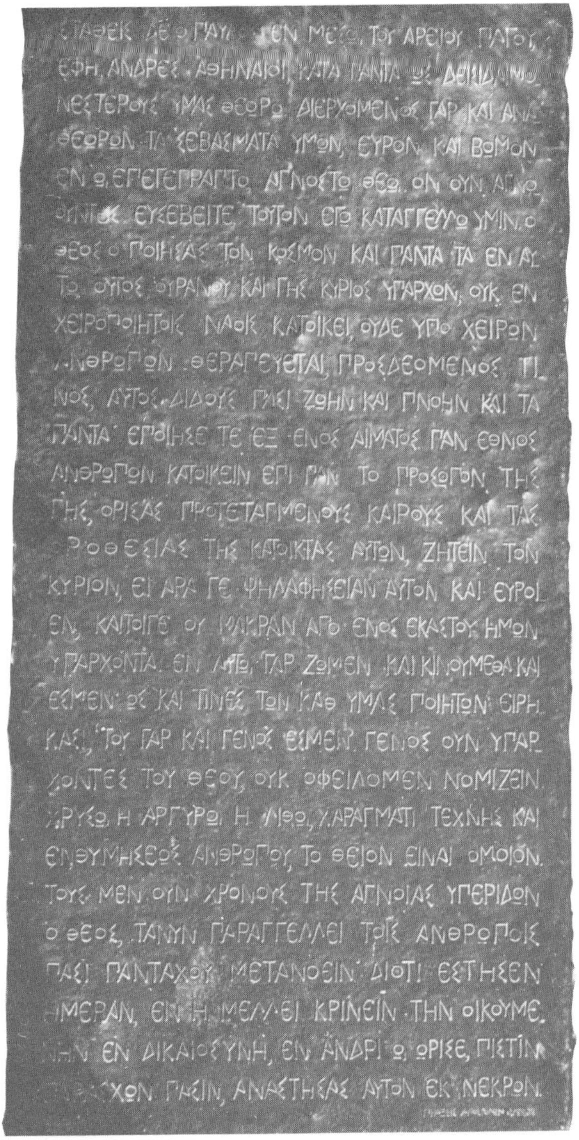

This plaque at the Areopagus
contains the Greek text of Paul's speech
before the city council at this site (Acts 17:22-31).

So they took Paul,
brought him before the city council,
the Areopagus, and said,
"We would like to know what this new teaching is
that you are talking about.
Some of the things we hear you say
sound strange to us,
and we would like to know what they mean."

ACTS 17:19-20

The city council, or Areopagus,
was made up of distinguished Athenians.
They took their name
from the place where they regularly met.
It was a rock hill next to the acropolis,
but slightly smaller.

Steps chiseled directly into the hill
led to the top.
There, on three sides, benches hewn from
the rock are still visible today.
In Paul's time,
the Areopagus concerned itself with matters
relating to education and religion.
It was before this council
that Paul was asked to speak about Jesus.

THE UNKNOWN GOD

Paul stood up in front of the city council
and said,
"I see that in every way you Athenians
are very religious.
For as I walked through your city
and looked at the places where you worship,
I found an altar on which is written,
'To an Unknown God.'
That which you worship, then,
even though you do not know it,
is what I now proclaim to you."

ACTS 17:22-23

Paul's approach to the Athenians
was open-minded.
He accepted their altar "To an Unknown God"
and used it as a bridge.
Such altars were widespread among ancients.
The traveler and geographer Pausanias,
who visited Athens in the second century,
reported seeing "altars to gods
named Unknown and of heroes."
Likewise, at Marathon, he reported seeing
an altar to "Unknown Gods."

Although none of these altars remains today,
archaeologists did unearth a comparable one
at Pergamum.
A corner of the description is missing,
but the complete version probably reads:
"To unknown gods, Capito, torch-bearer."

One explanation
for the popularity of such altars is traced to
the legend that Athens was once struck
by a plague that would not subside.
Not knowing which god could help them,
the Cretan poet Epimenides devised
an ingenious plan.

He let loose a flock of sheep in Athens.
Wherever a sheep grew tired and lay down,
there a sacrifice was offered
to the god whose altar or shrine was nearest.
If no altar or shrine was nearby,
the sacrifice was made to "an unknown god."
Legend has it that the plague ceased.

Paul used this "unknown god" as a bridge
to the God of Jesus Christ. He began:

"God, who made the world and everything in it,
is Lord of heaven and earth
and does not live in man-made temples.
Nor does he need anything
that we can supply by working for him,

since it is he himself
who gives life and breath and everything else
to everyone.
From one man he created all races of mankind
and made them live throughout the whole earth.
He himself fixed beforehand
the exact times and the limits of the places
where they would live.

He did this so that they would look for him,
and perhaps find him
as they felt around for him.
Yet God is actually not far from any one of us. . . .
It is as some of your poets have said,
'We too are his children.'. . .

"God has overlooked the times
when people did not know him,
but now he commands all of them everywhere
to turn away from their evil ways.
For he has fixed a day
in which he will judge the whole world
with justice by means of a man he has chosen.
He has given proof of this to everyone
by raising that man from death!"

ACTS 17:24-31

Again, Paul took a sympathetic approach.
To make the point that God is our Father,
he quoted from Aratus's *Natural Phenomena*.
There the early Stoic poet wrote:

Zeus fills the streets, the marts,
Zeus fills the seas, the shores, the rivers!
Everywhere our need is Zeus!
We also are his offspring!

RESPONSE

Paul's approach to his Gentile audience in Athens
stands in sharp contrast to Peter's approach
to his Jewish audience in Jerusalem.

City planners of Chicago and New York
were, ultimately, influenced by the grid designs
of Hippodamus of Miletus.
Piraeus, the port of Athens, shown here,
is a work of the fifth-century B.C. designer.

Peter's point of focus was Jesus who—

1 died and rose (Acts 3:15),
2 fulfilled the prophecies (3:18, 21ff),
3 is the promised Messiah (3:18, 20),
4 calls us to repentance (3:19),
5 will come again (3:21).

Paul's point of focus was God who—

1 made us (Acts 17:24),
2 preserves us (17:25),
3 leads us to seek him (17:27),
4 invites us to serve him (17:30),
5 will judge us through Jesus (17:31).

The Athenian response to Paul's words
is typical of the response
that people still make to the Good News:
some "made fun of Paul";
some "joined him and believed";
some procrastinated,
"We want to hear you speak about this again"
(Acts 17:32-34).

18 Bridge of Greece

Julius Caesar
rebuilt "twin-sea'd" Corinth in 44 B.C.
after it had lain in ruins for nearly a century.
It was in this city that Paul preached.

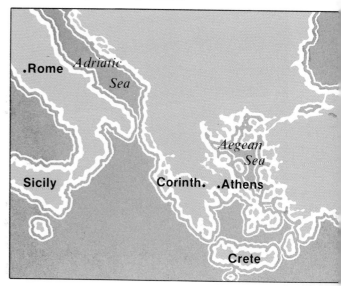

Horace, the ancient Latin poet,
dubbed Corinth the "twin-sea'd" city.
A glance at the map shows why.
It straddles a four-mile bridge of rocky land
that separates the Aegean Sea
from the Adriatic Sea.

The four-mile bridge also links
southern Greece and northern Greece.
This means that all north-south traffic
funneled through Corinth.

But Corinth's good luck didn't stop here.
Sailing around the tip of Greece
was so hazardous that ancient merchants
found it more profitable to go to Corinth.
There they would unload their cargo,
carry it across the bridge,
and reload to another ship on the other side.

Eventually, a *diolkos,* or "slipway,"
was built across the four-mile bridge.
Over it small ships were pulled
between the two gulfs.

Because of its ideal location,
Corinth became a great commercial hub
in the ancient world.

But Corinth paid a high price
for its popularity and prosperity.
It attracted a parade of unsavory characters:
fortune hunters, pleasure seekers, and degenerates.
Corinth developed a scandalous reputation
that is still remembered to this day.

Paul the Apostle
GIUSEPPE RICCIOTTI

*To a city like this Paul dared to go
and preach "Blessed are the poor . . . !
Blessed are the clean of heart . . . !"
What could this small and helpless David
expect to achieve against the armor-clad Goliath?
At the most, another failure, like that in Athens!
Notwithstanding all this
Paul was determined to try.*

These ancient stones were part of a *diolkos* ("slipway"). It was used for dragging small boats from Corinth's western Lechaeum harbor to its eastern Cenchrea harbor.

Swinging picks in the hot Corinth sun, 6,000 Jewish captives from the Judean War worked on the canal. This aerial view shows the canal today.

Digging the first dirt with a golden shovel,
Nero ordered a canal cut through
the four-mile bridge of rock
that separated Corinth's two harbors.

Begun about 15 years after Paul was there,
the project was soon abandoned.
Not until 1893 was the canal completed.
The Athens-Corinth railway bridge
spans the canal 170 feet above its waters.

He knew he would find corruption in Corinth
but not the arrogance and pride of Athens,
and he feared pride of the intellect
much more than pride of the flesh.

MIXED RECEPTION

Upon his arrival,
Paul learned of two recently arrived Jews,
Aquila and his wife, Priscilla.
They were victims of Emperor Claudius's edict
expelling all Jews from Rome.

Paul went to see them,
and stayed and worked with them,
because he earned his living
by making tents, just as they did.
He held discussions in the synagogue
every Sabbath, trying to convince
both Jews and Greeks.

ACTS 18:2–4

This pattern of living in Corinth continued
until Silas and Timothy rejoined Paul.

When Silas and Timothy arrived
from Macedonia, Paul gave his whole time
to preaching the message,
testifying to the Jews that Jesus is the Messiah.

ACTS 18:5

At first, Paul's work among the Jews
was fruitless and frustrating.
At one point
the situation became so hopeless that Paul
turned his back on the Jewish population.

He left them
and went to live in the house of a Gentile
named Titius Justus, who worshiped God;
his house was next to the synagogue.

ACTS 18:7

This stern course of action
caused Paul deep inner anguish and pain.
He loved his Jewish brothers and sisters
in a passionate way.
Touching on this in one of his letters,
Paul says:

How great is my sorrow,
how endless the pain in my heart
for my people, my own flesh and blood! . . .

How I wish with all my heart
that my own people might be saved!
How I pray to God for them!
I can assure you
that they are deeply devoted to God.

ROMANS 9:2–3; 10:1–2

Eventually,
Paul's praying and preaching bore fruit.

Crispus, who was the leader of the synagogue,
believed in the Lord, together with all his
family; and many other people in Corinth
heard the message, believed, and were baptized.

ACTS 18:8

105

But these conversions to Christianity
were but a small beginning.
For every believer in Corinth,
there were hundreds more who didn't believe,
especially among the Jewish population.

One night Paul had a vision
in which the Lord said to him,
"Do not be afraid, but keep on speaking
and do not give up, for I am with you.
No one will be able to harm you,
for many in this city are my people."
So Paul stayed there for a year and a half,
teaching the people the word of God.

ACTS 18:9–11

SERIOUS TROUBLE

This vision sustained Paul in the days ahead.
He continued his preaching among Jews
and Gentiles alike.
Paul's success among the Gentiles, especially,
did not go down well with many Jews.

When Gallio was made the Roman governor
of Achaia, the Jews got together,
seized Paul, and took him into court.
"This man," they said, "is trying to persuade
people to worship God in a way
that is against the law!"

Paul was about to speak
when Gallio said to the Jews,
"If this were a matter of some evil crime
or wrong that has been committed,
it would be reasonable for me
to be patient with you Jews.
But since it is an argument about words
and names and your own law,
you yourselves must settle it.
I will not be the judge of such things!"
And he drove them out of the court.

ACTS 18:12–16

106

City That Wouldn't Die

Earthquakes and wars
wiped out the city of Corinth three times.
Each time a new city rose from the ashes.

The most famous ruin from ancient Corinth
is the Temple of Apollo.
It was already 600 years old when Paul
stood in its shade to study its beauty.

The seven Doric columns that still stand
have a base diameter of six feet
and reach up twenty-five feet into the air.

The heart of Corinth
was its elegant public square, or agora.
It featured a variety of well-stocked shops,
shaded walkways, or stoa,
and a public judgment seat, called the bema.
It was to this bema that Paul was brought
to stand trial before Gallio (Acts 18:12).

Agora, or public square.
Ruins of the Temple of Apollo are visible
at the upper right.

Lechaion road,
leading south to the agora and the bema.
Paul walked this very road.

107

These fragments
were found in Delphi, in Greece.
They reproduce a letter of Tiberius Claudius
Caesar (name partially visible, upper left).
Referring to Gallio by name,
they assist in the dating of Paul's stay
in Corinth.

DEPARTURE

Paul stayed on with the believers in Corinth
for many days, then left them and sailed off
with Priscilla and Aquila for Syria. . . .
They arrived in Ephesus,
where Paul left Priscilla and Aquila.
He went into the synagogue
and held discussions with the Jews.
The people asked him to stay longer,
but he would not consent.
Instead, he told them as he left,
"If it is the will of God, I will come back to you."
And so he sailed from Ephesus.

When he arrived at Caesarea,
he went to Jerusalem and greeted the church,
and then went to Antioch.

ACTS 18:18-22

This episode with Gallio
helps us to pinpoint the exact date
of Paul's missionary work in Corinth.

An inscription found by archaeologists
at Delphi turned out to be a reproduction
of a letter from Claudius to the Delphinians.
From this Roman document we learn
that Gallio was proconsul of Achaia
after Emperor Claudius's 26th acclamation
(Roman armies gave this after major victories).
From related material,
we know that this acclamation took place
between January and August of A.D. 52.
Paul must have arrived in Corinth
around A.D. 50, staying until A.D. 52.

Paul's return to Antioch marks the end
of his so-called second missionary journey.
The time was late autumn, A.D. 52.

Ancient Copies

The oldest known copy of Paul's letters
dates from about A.D. 200.
Called the Chester Beatty Papyri,
it takes the form of a codex,
that is, individual sheets stacked in a pile.

Over the centuries
some of the sheets have become lost.
Missing letters from the Beatty Papyri are
the end of 1 Thessalonians,
all of 2 Thessalonians, 1-2 Timothy,
Titus, and Philemon.

Ancient letters were dictated to scribes.
Sometimes the scribes acted as secretaries;
that is, they phrased the letter as well as wrote it.
Paul used scribes often, as is clear from
1 Corinthians 16:21, 2 Thessalonians 3:17,
Galatians 6:11, Philemon 19, and Romans 16:22.

Writing was a major task in ancient times.
A student of papyrus letters estimates
that the 1,472 words of 1 Thessalonians
took ten sheets and twenty hours to write.
If this is correct, we can see
why Paul's letters sometimes
exhibit an unevenness in style, sudden jumps,
and occasional repetitions.

A problem arose
when parchment replaced papyrus
and the copying of biblical manuscripts
became widespread.
Well-meaning scribes sometimes updated
archaic words, rewrote awkward passages,
and inserted clarifications.

Scholars are now studying
some 4,000 ancient New Testament manuscripts
to try to produce an ideal master copy.

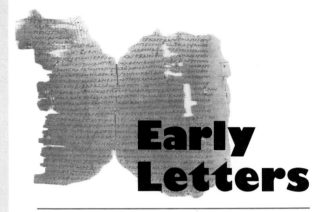

Early Letters

Tombs and sealed jars,
buried beneath the dry sands of Egypt,
have yielded up many ancient writings—
even personal letters.
One letter, scribbled on a scrap of papyrus,
is from a runaway boy.

I write to you that I am naked.
I beseech you, mother,
to be reconciled to me.
I know what I have brought upon myself. . . .
I know that I have sinned.

Soon the letter trails off,
too blurred and too frayed to read.

Few forms of writing can match letters,
for they are a window into the heart.
The letters of Paul are no exception.

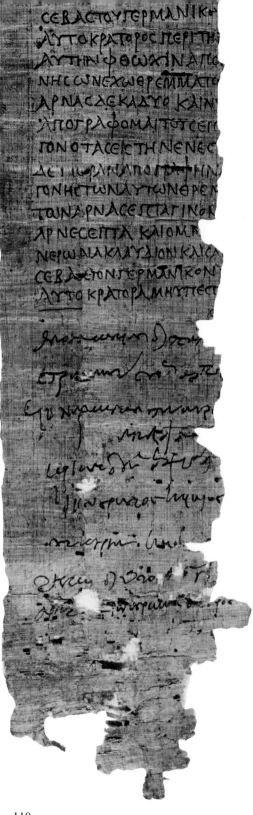

The Life of Paul
BENJAMIN WILLARD ROBINSON

In them we see not only Paul's thoughts
and opinions, but we see Paul himself
in all his greatness and intensity. . . .
As we read his letters
we can hear him calling insistently
through the megaphone of the centuries,
"I am not a book; I am a man."
He who truly reads his letters
sees not the pages and the ink
but looks through them
as through a window clear as crystal
into the house and home of Paul's soul.

Tradition attributes 13 letters to Paul.
They may be grouped as follows:

Early Letters: 1-2 Thessalonians
Great Letters: 1-2 Corinthians, Galatians,
                  Romans
Prison Letters: Philippians, Colossians,
                  Philemon, Ephesians
Pastoral Letters: 1-2 Timothy, Titus

I THESSALONIANS

A deep-down feeling stirred many people
around A.D. 50.
They felt something big was in the air.

Christians looked to the sky
for a sign of the Second Coming of Christ.
Jews looked to the hills
for some indication of the awaited Messiah.
Gentiles looked to their gods
for some relief from the tyrants of their day.

"It was one of those moments,"
wrote Hausrath in his six-volume work,
A History of New Testament Times,
"when the nations
stand in breathless expectation
of what the next hour will bring."

The First Letter to the Thessalonians
mirrors this expectation.
The immediate backdrop for the letter is this:

While Paul was preaching in Corinth,
news arrived that problems had arisen
in the Christian community at Thessalonica.
This was understandable,
because Paul was forced to leave the city
before completing instructions to his converts.

One problem
arose from the erroneous assumption
that the Christian community, as a whole,
would witness Jesus' Second Coming.
When some members of the community died,
the remaining members became disheartened.
Why should their friends and relatives
be deprived of the joy of seeing Jesus' coming?
Also, when was this coming going to occur?

With these questions in mind,
Paul sat down and composed a letter to them.
Here are some key excerpts from it.

From Paul, Silas, and Timothy—
To the people of the church in Thessalonica,
who belong to God the Father
and the Lord Jesus Christ:
May grace and peace be yours.

We always thank God for you all. . . .
Even though you suffered much . . .
you became an example to all believers
in Macedonia and Achaia. . . .

Our brothers, we want you to know the truth
about those who have died,
so that you will not be sad. . . .
Jesus died and rose again,
and so we believe
that God will take back with Jesus
those who have died believing in him. . . .

There is no need to write you . . .
about the times and occasions. . . .
For you yourselves know very well
that the Day of the Lord will come
as a thief comes at night. . . .

And so . . . be at peace among yourselves. . . .
We urge you . . . to warn the idle,
encourage the timid, help the weak,
be patient with everyone. . . .

Be joyful always, pray at all times,
be thankful in all circumstances. . . .
Read this letter to all the believers.

The grace of our Lord Jesus Christ be with you.

2 THESSALONIANS

Paul's first letter, apparently,
brought great joy to the Thessalonians.
In fact, it seems to have fueled expectations
about Jesus' coming.

Rumors began to fly.
Some members even quit their jobs.
This created a flurry of new problems.
Thus Paul wrote a second letter.

From Paul, Silas, and Timothy—
To the people of the church in Thessalonica,
who belong to God our Father
and the Lord Jesus Christ:
May God our Father and the Lord Jesus Christ
give you grace and peace. . . .

Volcanic ash froze these people of Pompeii
in the exact position they were in
when the disaster struck.
The plaster casts illustrate dramatically
Paul's warning about Jesus' Second Coming:

"The Day of the Lord will come
as a thief comes at night."

1 Thessalonians 5:2

Thief in the Night

Nineteen hundred years ago,
Pompeii was buried under volcanic ash.
Archaeologists are still digging up the city.
What they are finding is amazing:
carbonized loaves of bread,
fruit still retaining its flavor, and olives
still swimming in their oil.

Decayed bodies of people trapped in the disaster
have left hollow cavities in the hardened ash.
By pouring liquid plaster into these cavities,
archaeologists make casts of the victims.
Some of the casts evoke an emotional response.

One is a mother hugging her child tightly.
Another is a soldier clamped in stocks.
A third is a man standing upright,
with a sword locked in his hand.
His foot rests on a pile of gold and silver.
Scattered about him are five bodies,
probably would-be looters he had killed.

We must thank God at all times for you. . . .
We boast about the way you continue
to endure and believe. . . .

Concerning the coming of our Lord. . . .
Do not let anyone deceive you. . . .
For the Day will not come
until the final Rebellion takes place
and the Wicked One appears. . . .

Don't you remember?
I told you all this while I was with you.

Yet there is something
that keeps this from happening now,
and you know what it is. . . .

So then . . . hold on to those truths
which we taught you,
both in our preaching and in our letter. . . .

We hear that there are some people among you
who live lazy lives and who do nothing. . . .
We . . . warn them to lead orderly lives
and work to earn their own living. . . .

It may be that someone there
will not obey the message
we send you in this letter. . . .
But do not treat him as an enemy;
instead, warn him as a brother. . . .

With my own hand I write this:
Greetings from Paul. *This is the way*
I sign every letter; this is how I write.

May the grace of our Lord Jesus Christ
be with you all.

Paul's letter, evidently,
produced the desired effect,
for we hear of no further problems.

Paul's reply boils down to this:
Certain events
must first precede Jesus' Second Coming.
One of these is a major confrontation
between the forces of good and evil.
Paul's letter is vague about these events,
because he presumes his readers are familiar
with the teaching he gave to them orally
at an earlier date.

Whatever it is that keeps everything
from happening can only be guessed at.
Some have suggested the obstacle
is the preaching of the Gospel itself.
It must be proclaimed to all nations first.

FORMAT

Paul's two letters to the Thessalonians
illustrate the general format he used
in most letters,
which is the more or less fixed format
of most ancient Greco-Roman letters.

There is an opening salutation,
a thanksgiving, the body proper,
and a conclusion and final greeting.

The opening salutation consisted
of the sender's name, the recipient's name,
and a peace greeting.

The thanksgiving acted as a bridge
to the body and the theme of the letter.
But Paul introduced something totally original
to the traditional greeting.
He expanded it into a kind of prayer,
even including what appear to be excerpts
from early "eucharistic" liturgies.
Thus, 2 Corinthians 1:3 reads:

Let us give thanks
to the God and Father of our Lord Jesus Christ,
the merciful Father,
the God from whom all help comes!

Next followed the body of the letter.
It usually included two sections:
one treating truths of the Christian message,
the other giving instructions for Christian living.

The conclusion and final greeting
brought the letter to a close.
It frequently contained personal news,
instructions for certain individual Christians,
and the typical Pauline blessing:
"The grace of our Lord Jesus Christ
be with you" (1 Thessalonians 5:28).

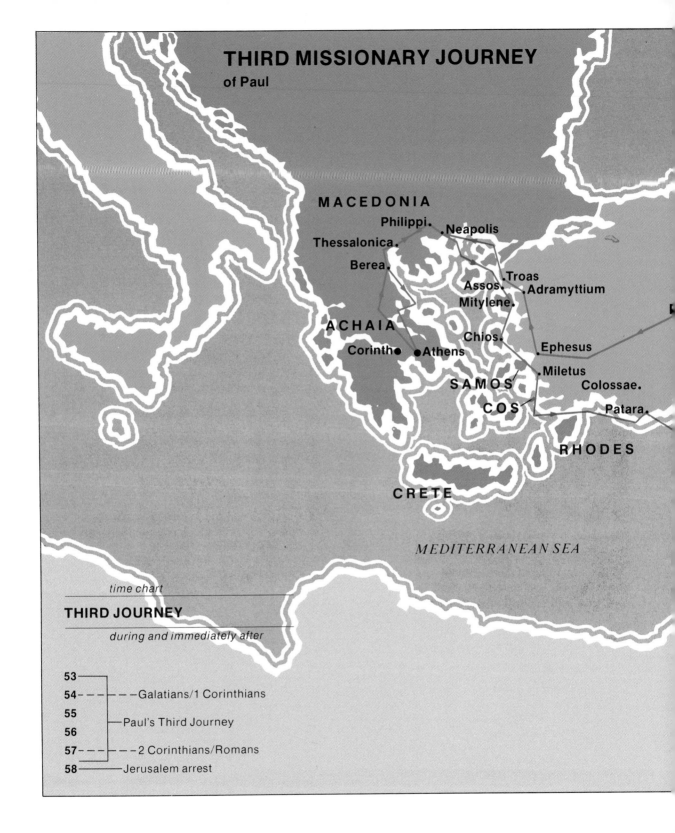

PART FIVE

THIRD MISSIONARY JOURNEY
of Paul

MACEDONIA

Philippi. .Neapolis

Thessalonica.

Berea. .Troas

Assos. .Adramyttium

Mitylene.

ACHAIA

Corinth. .Athens

Chios. .Ephesus

.Miletus

SAMOS

Colossae.

COS

Patara.

RHODES

CRETE

MEDITERRANEAN SEA

time chart

THIRD JOURNEY
during and immediately after

53
54 ———— Galatians/1 Corinthians
55
———— Paul's Third Journey
56
57 ———— 2 Corinthians/Romans
58 ———— Jerusalem arrest

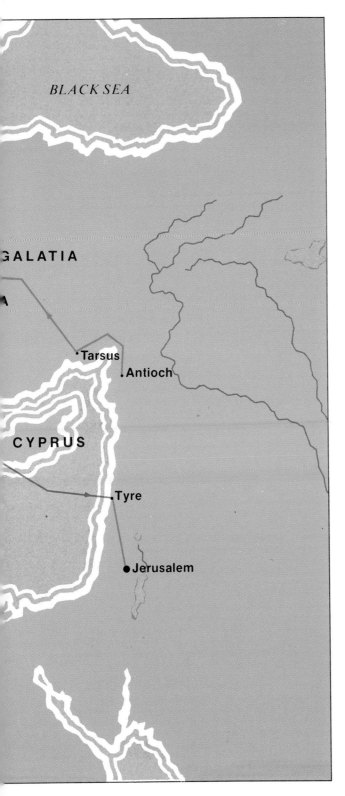

THIRD MISSIONARY JOURNEY

Acts 19-22

On the map:

BLACK SEA

GALATIA

A

•Tarsus

•Antioch

CYPRUS

•Tyre

•Jerusalem

19
Ephesus Riot

In his book *Dreams,*
Morton Kelsey tells of a missionary friend
who preached the message of Christianity
on the island of Bali.
The easiest person on the island to convert
was the witch doctor, or medicine man.
This prompted Kelsey to recall
an observation by publisher Jean Williams.

She said
that it was perfectly clear to her how Paul
could go to a community for only six weeks
and immediately leave behind
a body of believers.
All he had to do was to change
their allegiance to a different morality,
not to a different world view,
because they already believed
in a spiritual reality.

A prerequisite for accepting Christianity
is openness to spiritual reality.

For people open to spiritual reality,
that is, those having a spiritual mentality,
the process of presenting Christianity
is greatly facilitated.

For people insensitive to spiritual reality,
the process is greatly impeded.

Sometimes a spiritual mentality
can be laced with superstition and evil.
This was the case, as we shall see,
with the people in Ephesus,
where Paul planned to go
as he left Antioch on another mission trip.

Paul's first stop was in the Galatian country.
There he revisited the Christian communities
of Derbe, Lystra, and Iconium.
Apparently,
Paul was pleased with what he found,
since Luke says nothing else about the visit
except that Paul stopped there.

Paul's second stop was the Phyrgian country.
There he revisited the Christian communities
at Colossae, Laodicea, and Hierapolis.
Again, nothing else is said about the visit.

EPHESUS

Paul's third stop was the city of Ephesus.
When he got there,
he learned that he had been preceded
by a "half-Christian" named Apollos.

Apollos was an eloquent speaker
and had a thorough knowledge
of the Scriptures.
He had been instructed in the Way of the Lord,
and with great enthusiasm he proclaimed
and taught correctly the facts about Jesus.
However, he knew only the baptism of John.
He began to speak boldly in the synagogue.
When Priscilla and Aquila heard him,
they took him home with them
and explained to him more correctly
the Way of God.

ACTS 18:24-26

116

Looking like new,
this 2,000-year-old silver coin
shows the head of "Artemis of Ephesus"
(Acts 19:28).
The reverse shows a stag and a bee,
symbols of the goddess.

Digging has been going on in Ephesus
off and on since 1863.
Among the discoveries made by archaeologists
have been public baths, shops,
a library, and ancient streets.

This explains
why Paul found some people in Ephesus
who had been baptized with John's baptism
but not with the baptism of the Lord Jesus.
Paul explained to these people:

"The baptism of John
was for those who turned from their sins;
and he told the people of Israel
to believe in the one who was coming
after him—that is, in Jesus."

When they heard this, they were baptized
in the name of the Lord Jesus.
Paul placed his hands on them,
and the Holy Spirit came upon them;
they spoke in strange tongues
and also proclaimed God's message.

ACTS 19:4-6

OPPOSITION—AND JAIL?

Along with success came setbacks.

Paul went into the synagogue
and for three months spoke boldly
with the people, holding discussions with them
and trying to convince them
about the Kingdom of God.
But some of them were stubborn
and would not believe,
and before the whole group
they said evil things
about the Way of the Lord.

ACTS 19:8-9

Possibly, in connection with this situation,
Paul was briefly jailed in Ephesus.
Although Acts
says nothing about his being jailed,
Christian tradition affirms that he was.

118

HALL OF TYRANNUS

After Paul's confrontation at the synagogue,
he gave up his discussions there
and made arrangements to hold them elsewhere.

He held discussions in the . . . hall of Tyrannus.
This went on for two years,
so that all the people who lived in
the province of Asia, both Jews and Gentiles,
heard the word of the Lord.

ACTS 19:9-10

Tyrannus was quite possibly a teacher,
perhaps a philosopher.
No doubt,
he lectured during the cool morning hours,
leaving the hall to Paul afterward.
This would accord with a Greek manuscript
which contains the comment
that Paul taught between 11 A.M. and 5 P.M.

Most scholars would agree with this.
These were the hours
when the average Ephesian citizen
ate the noon meal and took a siesta.
Some commentators say that more Ephesians
were asleep at 1 P.M. than at 1 A.M.

In all probability,
Paul worked at his trade in the morning.
That Paul supported himself in Ephesus
is clear from a statement to Ephesian elders.

"You yourselves know
that I have worked with these hands of mine
to provide everything
that my companions and I have needed."

ACTS 20:34

This page of the so-called "magic papyrus of Paris" (ca. A.D. 300) preserves pagan and Jewish spells akin to those referred to in Acts 19:19.

Magic Spells

Roving exorcists were common in Paul's day, especially in places like Ephesus, where magic and superstition were widespread. In his *Comedy of Errors,* Shakespeare refers to Ephesus as the city of "dark-working sorcerers," "soul-killing witches," and "prating mountebanks."

Ancients used the term "Ephesus Writings" to refer to magical papyri or to magical formulae to be placed in lockets and worn around the neck. Archaeologists have found papyri scrolls that contain a number of exorcist rites. One ancient Jewish rite is reminiscent of the Acts episode. It reads:

Invocation to be uttered
over the head (of the possessed one).
Place before him branches of olive,
and standing behind him say:
"Hail, spirit of Abraham;
hail, spirit of Isaac; hail, spirit of Jacob;
Jesus the Christ, the holy one . . .
I adjure thee, O demon, whoever thou art. . . .
Come forth . . . and depart. . . .
I give you over to black chaos."

Greek Papyri, No. 47

WHO ARE YOU?

Another familiar pattern emerged: miracles began to accompany Paul's preaching. Soon his belongings began to disappear, as people took them to the sick and possessed, seeking a cure in the name of the Lord Jesus.

Some Jews who traveled around
and drove out evil spirits also tried to use
the name of the Lord Jesus to do this. . . .

But the evil spirit said to them,
"I know Jesus, and I know about Paul;
but you—who are you?"

The man who had the evil spirit in him
attacked them with such violence
that he overpowered them all.
They ran away from his house,
wounded and with their clothes torn off.

ACTS 19:13-16

The sophisticated humor of this story suggests that it was repeated many times around Christian dinner tables. Luke couldn't resist sharing it with his readers.

Luke identifies the traveling exorcists as sons of a Jewish high priest named Sceva. No high priest by that name is known. Possibly the title was so clearly outlandish that Luke repeats it for humor's sake.

The exorcism episode—
and the impact it had on the people—
ends with a remark that shows
that even Christians still dabbled in magic.

They were all filled with fear. . . .
Many of the believers came, publicly
admitting and revealing what they had done.
Many of those who had practiced magic
brought their books together and burned them.

ACTS 19:17-19

Mob Scene

A madman named Herostratus,
hoping to win a place in history books,
torched the great Temple of Artemis.
Tradition says
that very same night, in October 356 B.C.,
Alexander the Great was born.

Following the burning,
a newer and more spectacular temple was built.
It was this temple that Paul knew.
It stood until invaders sacked it in A.D. 262.
The temple's focal point was a great altar
behind which stood the statue of Artemis.

Paul's stay in Ephesus came to an end
following a near riot in the great theater
on the western slope of Mount Pion.

The mob gathered here.
About 500 feet in diameter,
the great theater held over 24,000 people.

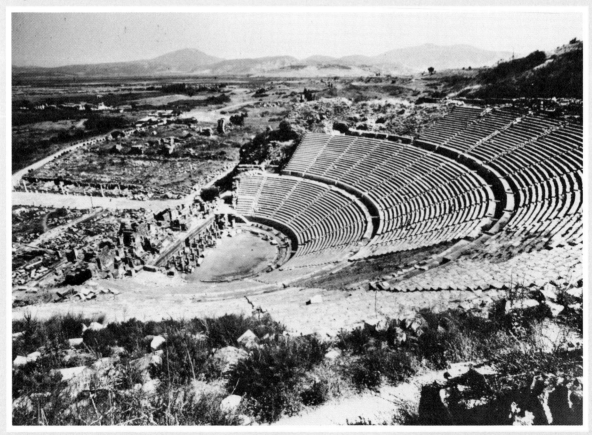

RIOT SITUATION

Paul's success in Ephesus
soon took its toll on the city's silversmiths.
Before Paul came to the city,
they had been doing a booming business
selling miniatures of the Temple of Artemis
and other objects to cult worshipers.
When Paul's preaching
began to cut into their business,
Demetrius called together the other smiths.

"There is the danger . . .
that this business of ours will get a bad name.
Not only that,
but there is also the danger
that the temple of the great goddess Artemis
will come to mean nothing
and that her greatness will be destroyed."

ACTS 19:27

The appeal of Demetrius was so forceful
that the smiths and other onlookers
began chanting:
"Great is Artemis of Ephesus!"

Soon, word buzzed throughout the city
that serious trouble was brewing
between Christians and worshipers of Artemis.
Within minutes,
the streets were swarming with spectators,
streaming excitedly toward the amphitheater—
the congregating place at times like this.

When Paul got news that two Christians,
Gaius and Aristarchus, were pounced upon
by the mob and paraded off to the theater,
he decided to go to their aid.
But some local officials who knew Paul
prevailed upon him to maintain a low profile.

Meanwhile the whole meeting was in an uproar:
some people were shouting one thing,
others were shouting something else,

because most of them did not even know
why they had come together.

ACTS 19:32

The situation went on for two hours
with the crowd chanting in rhythm,
"Great is Artemis of Ephesus!"
Finally, a city official was able to quiet the crowd.

"Fellow Ephesians!" he said.
"Everyone knows that the city of Ephesus
is the keeper of the temple of the great Artemis
and of the sacred stone
that fell down from heaven.
Nobody can deny these things.
So then, you must calm down. . . .

"If Demetrius and his workers
have an accusation against anyone,
we have the authorities
and the regular days for court;
charges can be made there.
But if there is something more that you want,
it will have to be settled
in a legal meeting of citizens. . . ."
After saying this, he dismissed the meeting.

ACTS 19:35-41

EPHESUS EXIT

In the light of this explosive episode,
Paul decided to leave Ephesus for a while
to let things cool down.

Paul called together the believers
and with words of encouragement
said good-bye to them.
Then he left and went on to Macedonia.

ACTS 20:1

From Macedonia,
Paul went on to Achaia (Corinth),
"where he stayed three months" (Acts 20:3).

20
Tears and Farewell

"To preach more than an hour,"
said George Whitefield,
"a man should be an angel himself
or have angels for hearers."

This was no less true for Paul.
At times he forgot and got carried away.
One of those times was in Troas.

TROAS

After Paul left Corinth, he went to Troas.
There he was rejoined by Luke.
Although the two missionaries stayed in Troas
only one week, it was long enough for Luke
to record one of the most delightful episodes
in Acts.

On Saturday evening
we gathered together for the fellowship meal.
Paul spoke to the people
and kept on speaking until midnight,
since he was going to leave the next day.
Many lamps were burning in the upstairs room
where we were meeting.
A young man named Eutychus
was sitting in the window,
and as Paul kept on talking,
Eutychus got sleepier and sleepier,
until he finally went sound asleep
and fell from the third story to the ground.
When they picked him up, he was dead.
But Paul went down and threw himself on him. . . .
"Don't worry," he said, "he is still alive!"
Then he went back upstairs, broke bread, and ate.
After talking with them for a long time,
even until sunrise, Paul left.
They took the young man home alive
and were greatly comforted.

ACTS 20:7-12

Few stories in Scripture are more vivid
and down-to-earth than this one.
Young Eutychus
was tired from a long day of work and play.
When the air became stuffy
from the many lamps burning in the room,
the boy moved over to an open window—
not made of glass but of hinged panels.
The rest of the story we know.
Paul was thrust into the role of an Elisha
(2 Kings 4:32-37).

LORD'S SUPPER

Early Christians followed the Jewish practice
of using sunset to divide their days.
In other words,
the Lord's Day began at sunset on Saturday.

Christians celebrated the Last Supper
on the Lord's Day within the framework
of a weekly fellowship meeting and meal.
Occasionally, these weekly gatherings
turned into unfit settings for worshiping
and celebrating the Lord's Supper.
Paul lashes out at the Corinthians:

I do not praise you,
because your meetings for worship
actually do more harm than good. . . .
For as you eat,
each one goes ahead with his own meal,
so that some are hungry
while others get drunk.

1 CORINTHIANS 11:17, 21

About the Lord's Supper itself,
which was celebrated as part of this meal,
Paul says:

I received from the Lord
the teaching that I passed on to you:
that the Lord Jesus,
on the night he was betrayed,
took a piece of bread,
gave thanks to God, broke it, and said,
"This is my body, which is for you.
Do this in memory of me."
In the same way,
after the supper he took the cup and said,
"This cup is God's new covenant,
sealed with my blood.
Whenever you drink it,
do so in memory of me." . . .

It follows
that if anyone eats the Lord's bread
or drinks from his cup
in a way that dishonors him,
he is guilty of sin
against the Lord's body and blood.

1 CORINTHIANS 11:23-27

Bread of Remembrance

"The horror of that moment,"
the King went on,
"I shall never, never, forget!"
"You will, though," the Queen said,
"if you don't make a memorandum of it."

Lewis Carroll

The Eucharist is the living memorandum
of Jesus' passion, death, and resurrection.
But it is not just a "mental" recalling;
it is a "sacra-mental" reliving.
There's a big difference.

The biblical understanding of remembering
is not looking backward into time
to recall an event,
but bringing the event forward into time
to relive it.
The biblical understanding of remembering
is a form of real participation.

Through ritual remembrance,
Israel brought the past into the present.
In this way, Jews of later times shared in
God's blessing to Jews of earlier times.
It is with this understanding
that Christians gather around the Lord's table
in response to Jesus' invitation:

"Do this in memory of me."

LUKE 22:19

From Assos,
Paul and Luke sailed to Mitylene (shown here)
on the island of Lesbos.
Sardine fishing has been a centuries-old
occupation for the islanders.

Haunting Spirit

Miletus is a ghost town today.
Only fragmentary traces
of an ancient civilization keep vigil.
Yet, a haunting spirit lives on at the site,
as the following incident shows.

Some years ago, BBC-TV in England
hired a journalist and a biblical expert
to retrace Paul's footsteps.
With cameras rolling,
film crews tagged along with the two men.
After the project was completed,
the TV journalist wrote a letter of thanks
to the biblical expert.
In it, he recalled one site, in particular,
that had moved them both deeply.

Paul: Envoy Extraordinary
MALCOLM MUGGERIDGE AND ALEC VIDLER

*We sensed Paul's presence more strongly
than anywhere else
in that desolate stretch of marshland,
once Miletus' harbour. . . .
Perhaps it was the virtual absence of ruins
and of tourists . . .
but as you read the speech to the elders
about how they would see his face no more,
and how he commended them to God . . .
I felt like joining them in weeping. . . .
So I shall always think of him there.*

The harbor of Miletus
began its decline in the Middle Ages
when silt invaded its harbor
and began filling it up.

FINAL VISIT

After the Eutychus event, Paul and Luke
began their long journey back to Jerusalem.
Along the way, they stopped at Assos
and at Miletus
for a visit with Christian elders.
The meeting was emotion packed,
with Paul sharing what was in his heart.

"I am going to Jerusalem,
not knowing what will happen to me there.
I only know that in every city
the Holy Spirit has warned me
that prison and troubles wait for me.
But I reckon my own life
to be worth nothing to me;
I only want to complete my mission
and finish the work
that the Lord Jesus gave me to do. . . .

"Keep watch over yourselves
and over all the flock which the Holy Spirit
has placed in your care. . . .
I know that after I leave,
fierce wolves will come among you,
and they will not spare the flock. . . .

"And now I commend you
to the care of God . . . remembering the
words that the Lord Jesus himself said,
'There is more happiness in giving
than in receiving.'"

When Paul finished,
he knelt down with them and prayed.
They were all crying as they hugged him
and kissed him good-bye.
They were especially sad because he had said
that they would never see him again.
And so they went with him to the ship.

ACTS 20:22-38

21 Storm Brewing

Jimmy Stewart, the famous actor,
enlisted in the Air Corps in World War II.
Just before his bomber squadron flew overseas,
Jimmy's father visited him.

As the moment of departure neared,
Jimmy sensed that his father
was searching for something special to say.
But the words never came out.
The two embraced, parted, and waved.
Only later did Jimmy realize
that his father had slipped an envelope
into his pocket.
That night, when he was alone in his bunk,
he opened the envelope and read:

"This Was My Father"
JAMES STEWART
AS TOLD TO FLOYD MILLER

My dear Jim boy,
Soon after you read this letter,
you will be on your way
to the worst sort of danger. . . .
I am banking on
the enclosed copy of the 91st Psalm.

126

The thing that takes the place of fear and worry
is the promise in these words. . . .
I can say no more
I love you more than I can tell you.

Dad

Jimmy's father
never told him before that he loved him.
Jimmy wept.

In the envelope was a small booklet
with the words of Psalm 91:

Whoever goes to the LORD for safety,
whoever remains under the protection
of the Almighty, can say to him,
"You are my defender and protector.
You are my God; in you I trust." . . .

He will cover you with his wings;
you will be safe in his care;
his faithfulness will protect and defend you. . . .
God will put his angels in charge of you
to protect you wherever you go. . . .

PAUL'S PARTINGS

Paul's farewells
to his own "spiritual" sons and daughters
were emotional experiences, also.
One of the most moving was at Miletus,
but an even more moving one lay ahead.
Luke says of the trip from Miletus:

After sailing straight across, we came to Cos;
the next day we reached Rhodes,
and from there we went on to Patara.
There we found a ship
that was going to Phoenicia [Tyre]. . . .

We went ashore at Tyre,
where the ship was going to unload its cargo.
There we found some believers
and stayed with them a week.
By the power of the Spirit

Fallen Giant

A huge bronze nude of Apollo
once stood guard over the harbor of Rhodes.
Then an earthquake
sent it crashing into the sea in 224 B.C.

In the Steps of St. Paul
H. V. MORTON

When St. Paul came to Rhodes,
he must have seen this mass of bronze
lying at the entrance to the harbour,
just as Pliny saw it
when he visited the island in the same century.

"Even as it lies," wrote Pliny,
"it excites our wonder and imagination.
Few men can clasp the thumb in their arms,
and the fingers are larger than most statues."

The great fallen god
lay there in a heap until A.D. 656
when Saracens conquered the island
and sold the great metal chunks
to a junk dealer.

they told Paul not to go to Jerusalem.
But when our time with them was over,
we left and went on our way.
All of them, together with their wives
and children, went with us out of the city
to the beach, where we all knelt and prayed.
Then we said good-bye to one another,
and we went on board the ship
while they went back home.

ACTS 21:1–6

After a day's journey along the coast,
the ship came to Caesarea.
Paul and Luke gathered their few belongings
and set off on foot to the home of Philip,
a Christian living in Caesarea.
Describing the stay at Philip's home, Luke writes:

We had been there for several days
when a prophet named Agabus
arrived from Judea.
He came to us, took Paul's belt, tied up
his own feet and hands with it, and said,
"This is what the Holy Spirit says:
The owner of this belt will be tied up in this way
by the Jews in Jerusalem,
and they will hand him over to the Gentiles."

ACTS 21:10–11

127

Paul was undaunted, saying:

*"I am ready not only to be tied up
in Jerusalem but even to die there
for the sake of the Lord Jesus."*

ACTS 21:13

Shortly afterward,
Luke and Paul bade emotional farewells to all
and set out for Jerusalem

JERUSALEM

*When we arrived in Jerusalem,
the believers welcomed us warmly.
The next day Paul went with us to see James;
and all the church elders were present.
Paul greeted them and gave a complete report
of everything that God had done
among the Gentiles through his work.
After hearing him, they all praised God.*

ACTS 21:17-20

Then the believers told Paul of the trouble
brewing in Jerusalem among Jewish Christians.

*"They have been told
that you have been teaching all the Jews
who live in Gentile countries
to abandon the Law of Moses,
telling them not to circumcise their children
or follow the Jewish customs.
They are sure to hear that you have arrived."*

ACTS 21:21-22

The Jerusalem leaders
urged Paul to demonstrate in some clear way
that he respected Jewish tradition. They said:

*"This is what we want you to do.
There are four men here who have taken a vow.
Go along with them and join them
in the ceremony of purification."*

ACTS 21:23-24

Paul went along with their proposal
because the ceremony, as such,
did not compromise his position on Gentiles.
It was only a "devotional" practice
which, in fact, Paul himself seems to have
performed before leaving Corinth (Acts 18:18).

It was hoped that Paul's action
would demonstrate to his critics
that he was not opposed to Jewish Christians
retaining certain traditional Jewish practices.
Rather, he was opposed to imposing
these Jewish practices on Gentile Christians.

*So Paul took the men
and the next day performed the ceremony
of purification with them.
Then he went into the Temple
and gave notice of how many days it would be
until the end of the period of purification,
when a sacrifice would be offered
for each one of them.*

ACTS 21:26

For the time being,
an emotional confrontation was avoided.
Paul hoped he could buy enough time
to reduce the inner tensions and feelings
of Jewish Christians so that discussion
and better understanding might prevail.

22

The Storm Strikes

Twenty political prisoners stood helplessly
in the public square in St. Petersburg, Russia.

The first three were blindfolded quickly
and placed before a firing squad.
Just as the commanding officer prepared
to bark "Fire!" a messenger charged up.
Emperor Nicholas I had just commuted
their sentences from death to hard labor.

One of the prisoners saved by the reprieve
was Feodor Dostoevski.
He would go on to write some of the greatest
literature ever to appear in Russian.

Paul had a similar narrow escape from death.
It took place at the hands of a lynch mob
in Jerusalem, when some of his opponents
accused him of defiling the temple
by bringing a Gentile into it.

*The people all ran together, grabbed Paul,
and dragged him out of the Temple. . . .
The mob was trying to kill Paul,
when a report was sent up to the commander
of the Roman troops
that all of Jerusalem was rioting.
At once the commander took some officers
and soldiers and rushed down to the crowd.
When the people saw him with the soldiers,
they stopped beating Paul.
The commander went over to Paul,
arrested him, and ordered him to be bound
with two chains.
Then he asked, "Who is this man,
and what has he done?"*

ACTS 21:30-33

The Tower of Antonia, a Roman fortress,
overlooked the temple plaza.
Here, well-trained soldiers stood guard
monitoring the milling crowds.
When an alert lookout spotted the flare-up,
he called the commander, and soldiers came
to cap the explosive situation before it spread.

PAUL'S DEFENSE

The commander
took Paul into immediate custody,
probably for Paul's own protection.
Then Paul made a surprising request.
He asked to address the mob.
The commander was agreeable.

*So Paul stood on the steps
and motioned with his hand for the people
to be silent.
When they were quiet,
Paul spoke to them in Hebrew. . . .*

*When they heard him speaking to them
in Hebrew, they became even quieter;
and Paul went on:*

129

This excavated warning sign
was fixed to the stone barrier dividing
the outer temple court from the inner ones.
It warned that any Gentile going beyond
this point would be punished by death.

Paul was accused of being party
to such an offense (Acts 21:28).
Later, Paul referred to the temple barrier
in Ephesians 2:14.
This sign, found by Clermont-Genneau
in 1871, is now in an Istanbul museum.

The Western (Wailing) Wall
is all that remains of the Jerusalem temple
which Paul knew and loved.
This wall formed part of the plaza
upon which the temple once stood.

When Israeli tanks
rumbled into Jerusalem's Old City in 1967,
it was the first time,
but for a brief period in A.D. 135,
that Jews controlled the site since A.D. 70.

130

"I am a Jew, born in Tarsus in Cilicia,
but brought up here in Jerusalem
as a student of Gamaliel.
I received strict instruction in the Law
of our ancestors and was just as dedicated
to God as are all of you who are here today.
I persecuted to the death
the people who followed this Way. . . .
The High Priest and the whole Council
can prove that I am telling the truth.
I received from them letters
written to fellow Jews in Damascus,
so I went there to arrest these people
and bring them back in chains to Jerusalem
to be punished."

ACTS 21:40–22:5

Paul then recounted
his experience on the road to Damascus
and how it led to his conversion.
He continued:

"I went back to Jerusalem,
and while I was praying in the Temple,
I had a vision, in which I saw the Lord,
as he said to me,
'Hurry and leave Jerusalem quickly,
because the people here will not accept
your witness about me. . . .
I will send you far away to the Gentiles.'"

ACTS 22:17–21

THE EXPLOSION

The people
listened to Paul until he said this;
but then they started shouting
at the top of their voices,
"Away with him! Kill him! He's not fit to live!"
They were screaming, waving their clothes,
and throwing dust up in the air.

ACTS 22:22–23

Paul's reference to the Gentiles
sent the crowd into a wild frenzy.
It was obvious that there was something more
to the situation than met the eye.

The Roman commander ordered his men
to take Paul into the fort,
and he told them to whip him
in order to find out
why the Jews were screaming like this against him.

ACTS 22:24

The purpose
of whipping Paul was not to punish him.
Rather, it was a common way used by ancients
to extract information from a suspect.

But when they had tied him up to be whipped,
Paul said to the officer standing there,
"Is it lawful for you to whip a Roman citizen
who hasn't even been tried for any crime?". . .

At once the men who were going to question Paul
drew back from him;
and the commander was frightened
when he realized that Paul was a Roman citizen
and that he had put him in chains.

ACTS 22:25, 29

Taking a quick inventory of the situation,
the commander decided
to keep Paul in Roman custody for the night.
In the morning,
he would ask the Sanhedrin (Jewish Council)
to review the entire case.

For the time being Paul was safe;
but even greater dangers lay ahead for him.

Great Letters

Sydney Piddington
was 19 when he was captured in World War II.
He was imprisoned in Changeli in Singapore,
with other Australian POWs.
One thing that helped him survive the long hours
was Lin Yutang's book *The Importance of Living.*
It is the kind of book that you don't just read;
you meditate on what it says.

The same kind of provocative reading
Piddington found in Lin Yutang's book
is also found in Paul's "great letters":
1-2 Corinthians, Galatians, Romans.
These letters are called "great"
because of their profound ideas and teaching.

1 Corinthians and Galatians were probably written
from Ephesus (1 Corinthians 16:8).
2 Corinthians was probably written from Macedonia
(2 Corinthians 8:1).
Romans was probably written from Achaia (Corinth)
(Romans 15:26).

I CORINTHIANS

Greek dramatists
portrayed Corinthians in their plays
as drunk, depraved, and boisterous.

In Koine Greek, the word *korinthiazien*
means "to behave like a Corinthian,"
that is, in an immoral way.
The phrase *kore korinthe,* "Corinthian girl,"
was the accepted label for a prostitute.

Judging from his first letter,
some of Paul's Christian converts at Corinth
fitted the Corinthian stereotype.
Paul writes:

*Few of you were wise or powerful
or of high social standing.
God purposely chose
what the world considers nonsense
in order to shame the wise,
and he chose what the world considers weak
in order to shame the powerful.*
1 CORINTHIANS 1:26-27

It is understandable under the circumstances
that some of the Corinthians would fall back,
occasionally, into their old ways. Paul writes:

*Now, it is actually being said
that there is sexual immorality among you
so terrible that not even the heathen
would be guilty of it. . . .
You must remove the old yeast of sin
so that you will be entirely pure.*
1 CORINTHIANS 5:1, 7

Paul continues:

*Don't you know
that your body is a temple of the Holy Spirit,
who lives in you
and who was given to you by God?
You do not belong to yourselves but to God;*

This ancient sign from a Corinthian shop
contains the word *macellum* ("meat market").
(See lower left fragment.)
This is the same word in Latin used by Paul
in Greek (1 Corinthians 10:25), when he says,
"You are free to eat
anything sold in the meat market."

This hand-carved inscription,
found in Corinth,
is damaged but decipherable (e.g., HEBR).
It translates "Synagogue of the Hebrews."
Experts date it somewhere between
100 B.C. and A.D. 200.
The low quality of the carving
suggests a poor congregation
in accord with the one Paul describes
in 1 Corinthians 1:26.

he bought you for a price.
So use your bodies for God's glory.

1 CORINTHIANS 6:19-20

Another problem among the Corinthians
was division within the congregation.
Paul writes bluntly:

Some people from Chloe's family
have told me quite plainly . . .
that there are quarrels among you.
Let me put it this way:
each one of you says something different.
One says, "I follow Paul";
another, "I follow Apollos";
another, "I follow Peter";
and another, "I follow Christ." . . .

When one of you says, "I follow Paul,"
and another, "I follow Apollos"—
aren't you acting like worldly people?

1 CORINTHIANS 1:11-12; 3:4

Later in the letter,
Paul uses this striking image to illustrate
the unity that should exist among Christians:

Christ is like a single body,
which has many parts; it is still one body,
even though it is made up of different parts.
In the same way, all of us,
whether Jews or Gentiles,
whether slaves or free,
have been baptized into the one body
by the same Spirit. . . .

"... timber from Oregon...."

Prayer of a Doodler

"Prayer on a Pencil"
MAX PAULI

I was just sitting here, Lord,
doodling with my pencil,
when it struck me as something strange.
Here was a sharpened lead pencil,
common to me since kindergarten,
yet odd at the same time.
It was graphite from Pennsylvania,
timber from Oregon,
rubber from Brazil,
all stamped together in one instrument
intended for my personal use.
It was all those people
in all those places—
down in coal mines,
high up in mountains,
deep in steaming jungles,
digging, cutting, tapping—
striving together for my comfort,
so I could doodle and scratch sentences.
Lord, if so many separate human beings
can work together to produce something
so slight as a pencil,
why can't we work together
to create something more significant,
like universal love or world peace?

And so there is no division in the body,
but all its different parts
have the same concern for one another.
If one part of the body suffers,
all the other parts suffer with it....

All of you are Christ's body,
and each one is a part of it.

1 CORINTHIANS 12:12–13, 25–27

Paul concludes his call for unity
by dramatizing the importance of love.
He writes:

I may have the gift of inspired preaching;
I may have all knowledge and understand
all secrets;
I may have all the faith needed
to move mountains—
but if I have no love, I am nothing.
I may give away everything I have,
and even give up my body to be burned—
but if I have no love, this does me no good.

Love is patient and kind;
it is not jealous or conceited or proud;
love is not ill-mannered or selfish or irritable;
love does not keep a record of wrongs;
love is not happy with evil,
but is happy with the truth.
Love never gives up.... Love is eternal.

1 CORINTHIANS 13:2–8

"Just as all people die
because of their union with Adam,
in the same way all will be raised to life
because of their union with Christ....
Just as we wear
the likeness of the man made of earth,
so we will wear
the likeness of the Man from heaven."
1 Corinthians 15:22, 49

134

2 CORINTHIANS

1 Corinthians 5:9
refers to an earlier letter Paul wrote.
Since we have no trace of it,
some biblical scholars call it the "lost letter."

Likewise, 2 Corinthians 2:4 refers to
a sad letter written with "many tears."
Since this does not seem to be 1 Corinthians,
some call it the second "lost letter" of Paul.

Still others propose a fascinating solution
to the "lost letters."
They start by pointing out the uneven style
and the disjointed pattern of 2 Corinthians.

For example, 2 Corinthians 6:14-7:1
not only interrupts the flow of the letter
but also advises a "separatist" relationship
that was followed earlier in Corinth
(1 Corinthians 5:9-12).
Could this be part of the first "lost letter"?

Similarly, the sharp tone of 2 Corinthians 10-13
clashes somewhat with the rest of the letter.
Could it be part of the second "lost letter"?

Some answer yes to both questions.
They think 2 Corinthians is a "collection"
of letters, rather than a single letter.

The Life of Paul
BENJAMIN WILLARD ROBINSON

Apparently one of Paul's disciples,
going around after the death of the apostle
with the object of making a collection,
and coming to Corinth,
found one long letter which would just about fill
a standard papyrus roll.
After copying the letter
he would number this roll Corinthians I.
Then using a second roll of papyrus
he arranged the shorter letters or fragments
as best he could, copied them, and numbered
the roll Corinthians II.

Among the striking passages
in Paul's Second Letter to the Corinthians
are the following.
Of his own suffering, Paul says:

The God and Father of our Lord Jesus Christ . . .
helps us in all our troubles,
so that we are able to help others . . .
using the same help
that we ourselves have received from God.

2 CORINTHIANS 1:3-4

135

"Some people conceive of the moon
as a magical and romantic object in the sky;
others think of it as a holy place.
Actually, it has all these elements. . . .
I cannot imagine a holier place."

Astronaut Jim Irwin

Inner Flight

Jim Irwin's moon voyage aboard *Apollo 15*
changed his life forever.
He writes in *To Rule the Night:*

*I wish I had been a writer or a poet,
so that I could convey more adequately
the feeling of this flight. . . .*

*It has been
sort of a slow-breaking revelation for me.
The ultimate effect
has been to deepen and strengthen
all the religious insight I ever had.
It has remade my faith. . . .
On the moon the total picture
of the power of God and His Son Jesus Christ
became abundantly clear to me.*

Irwin's insight recalls Paul's revelation.

*I know a certain Christian man
who fourteen years ago
was snatched up to the highest heaven . . .
and there he heard things
which cannot be put into words.*

2 CORINTHIANS 12:2–4

Encouraging the Corinthians
to give whatever financial aid they can
to the needy church of Jerusalem, Paul says:

*Remember that the person . . .
who plants many seeds will have a large crop.
Each one should give, then, as he has decided,
not with regret or out of a sense of duty;
for God loves the one who gives gladly.*

2 CORINTHIANS 9:6–7

Finally, about a "physical ailment"
that continually plagued him, Paul says:

*Three times I prayed to the Lord
about this and asked him to take it away.
But his answer was:
"My grace is all you need,
for my power is greatest when you are weak."
I am most happy, then,
to be proud of my weaknesses,
in order to feel the protection of Christ's
power over me.
I am content with weaknesses, insults,
hardships, persecutions, and difficulties
for Christ's sake.
For when I am weak, then I am strong.*

2 CORINTHIANS 12:8–10

GALATIANS

You don't keep the scaffolding in place
once the building has been erected.
That's pretty much Paul's argument
concerning the Mosaic Law,
when Christianity came of age.

Many Jewish converts to Christianity
did not interpret the Law as Paul did,
especially when it came to circumcision.
These "Judaizers," as they came to be called,
followed Paul into new Christian communities
and tried to upset his new converts.

Wounded Healer

They are chopping me up
and throwing me piece by piece into the grave.

That's what a minister told his close friend
after losing both legs
from injuries received in World War II.
Understandably, the minister was unable
to continue his work as pastor.

The loss of his pulpit
was as painful as the loss of his legs.
At first
he felt trapped and useless
in his wheelchair.
Then, slowly,
something unexpected happened—
he discovered a whole new ministry.

Doctors asked him
to talk with patients facing
similar operations.
Grace came to him
in the form of having to encourage others....
And in the process he was healed.

Robert M. Herhold

"The God and Father
of our Lord Jesus Christ . . .
helps us in all our troubles,
so that we are able to help others . . .
using the same help
that we ourselves have received from God."
2 Corinthians 1:3–4

They accused Paul of a "human" gospel,
at odds with the Gospel
preached by Peter, James, and John.

When Paul heard this was going on in Galatia
(Derbe, Lystra, Iconium, and Pisidian Antioch),
he fired off an emotion-packed letter
to his Galatian converts.

I am surprised at you!
In no time at all you are deserting the one
who called you by the grace of Christ. . . .

Let me tell you . . .
that the gospel I preach is not of human origin. . . .
It was Jesus Christ himself who revealed it to me.

GALATIANS 1:6, 11–12

As for being at odds with Peter, James,
and John, Paul says they commissioned him
to preach to Gentiles,
while they concentrated on preaching to Jews
(Galatians 2:9).

Paul then explains the bridgelike
relationship between the Law and Christ.
The Law's purpose was to reveal to people
their sinfulness and their need to be saved.
It was thus a stepping-stone to Christ.
Paul writes:

What, then, was the purpose of the Law?
It was added in order to show
what wrongdoing is, and it was meant to last
until the coming of Abraham's descendant. . . .

And so the Law was in charge of us
until Christ came. . . .
Now that the time for faith is here,
the Law is no longer in charge of us. . . .

You were baptized into union with Christ,
and now you are clothed, so to speak,
with the life of Christ himself.

GALATIANS 3:19, 24–27

Paul concludes
by exhorting the Galatians to live in accord
with their new life in Christ.
He says, for example:

If someone thinks he is something
when he really is nothing,
he is only deceiving himself.
Each one should judge his own conduct.
If it is good, then he can be proud
of what he himself has done,
without having to compare it
with what someone else has done. . . .

A person will reap exactly what he plants.
If he plants in the field of his natural desires,
from it he will gather the harvest of death;
if he plants in the field of the Spirit,
from the Spirit
he will gather the harvest of eternal life.

GALATIANS 6:3–8

Impossible Dream

The musical *Man of La Mancha*
was inspired by the life and work of Cervantes.
Born and raised in the midst of cruel poverty,
he became a soldier and was captured
in the Battle of Lepanto.
He was sentenced to years of slavery in Africa.
Broken in body, if not spirit, he died in 1616,
after completing his major work, *Don Quixote.*

Near the end of the musical, Quixote is dying.
At his side is Aldonza, a worthless woman
whom he had idealized and called Dulcinea.
Quixote loved her with a pure love,
unlike anything she had previously experienced.

When Quixote breathes his last,
Aldonza begins to sing "The Impossible Dream."
As the last echo of the song dies away,
someone shouts to her, "Aldonza."
She responds, "My name is Dulcinea."
With Quixote, Aldonza had died,
and Quixote's Dulcinea began to live in her.

I have been put to death with Christ on his cross,
so that it is no longer I who live,
but it is Christ who lives in me.
This life that I live now,
I live by faith in the Son of God,
who loved me and gave his life for me.

GALATIANS 2:19-20

ROMANS

In Corinth in A.D. 57,
Paul often walked down to the waterfront
to look at ships in the harbor.

When Paul spotted a ship from Rome,
his desires inevitably winged westward,
not only to Rome but even to Spain
(Romans 15:28).

But visiting Rome
was out of the question for the present.
So Paul did the next best thing.
He wrote a letter to the Christians there.

One of Paul's purposes in writing
was to steel them against being misled
by Judaizers, like those in Galatia.
Paul wanted them to understand
that Christianity did more than just fulfill
Judaism; it superseded it.

This damaged inscription from Old Corinth
probably read: "Erastus, in appreciation
of his 'public service' appointment,
laid this pavement at his own expense."
Some wonder if this could be the same Erastus
of whom Paul wrote in Romans 16:23:
"Erastus, the city treasurer,
and our brother Quartus send you their greetings."

139

Jewish Christians had just returned to Rome
after having been expelled from the city
by an edict of Claudius (A.D. 41-54, Acts 18.2).
Nero (A.D. 54-68) revoked the edict.

Paul's Letter to the Romans
is one of the best statements of Christianity
to be found in his writings.
The letter follows this general format:

1:18-3:20	the world before Christ,
3:21-5:21	the world after Christ,
6:1-8:39	new life in Christ,
9:1-11:36	God's plan for Israel,
12:1-15:13	Christian witness in the world.

Paul begins his letter
with a creedlike statement about Christ.

The Good News was promised long ago
by God through his prophets,
as written in the Holy Scriptures.
It is about his Son, our Lord Jesus Christ:
as to his humanity,
he was born a descendant of David;
as to his divine holiness,
he was shown with great power
to be the Son of God by being raised from death.
                              ROMANS 1:2-4

Paul continues
with a creedlike statement about salvation.

The gospel reveals
how God puts people right with himself:
it is through faith from beginning to end.
As the scripture says, "The person
who is put right with God through faith shall live."
                              ROMANS 1:17

Next, after pointing out how God
revealed himself to all through his creation
(Romans 1:20-23),

Paul uses the word of Psalm 14
to describe how all ignored God's revelation.

"There is no one who is righteous. . . .
They have all gone wrong;
no one does what is right, not even one."
                              ROMANS 3:10-12

Christ's coming reversed all this.

So then, as the one sin [Adam's sin]
condemned all mankind . . .
the one righteous act [Christ's death]
sets all mankind free and gives them life.
                              ROMANS 5:18

Since Christ has freed us,
we ought to conform our lives to his.

By our baptism, then, we were buried with him
and shared his death, in order that,
just as Christ was raised from death . . .
so also we might live a new life. . . .

Sin must no longer rule in your mortal bodies,
so that you obey the desires
of your natural self. . . .

To be controlled by human nature
results in death; to be controlled by the Spirit
results in life and peace.
                              ROMANS 6:4, 12; 8:6

Finally, Paul touches on God's plan for Israel.
He expresses the conviction that the Israelites
will eventually find their way
into the kingdom (Romans 11:25-29).

Paul ends by exhorting Christians
to let God take over their lives completely.

Do not conform yourselves
to the standards of this world,
but let God transform you inwardly
by a complete change of your mind.
                              ROMANS 12:2

No Workbench

A *Peanuts* cartoon serves as a parable
to illustrate the hopeless plight of humanity
before Jesus entered the world.

The first picture of the cartoon
shows Charlie Brown staring at a tool box.
He is saying something like this:
"I can't do it! I can't do it!"
The second picture shows Lucy entering.
She says something like this:
"What's wrong, Charlie? You seem unhappy."
The last picture has Charlie answer Lucy:
"I *am* unhappy! I want to build a workbench,
but I don't have a workbench to build it on."

The cartoon's point, when applied to Jesus,
is clear: Jesus gave humanity
a starting point for rebuilding all things.
Augustine stressed the importance of Jesus
this way:

We would be unhappy forever,
had it not been for Jesus' mercy. . . .
We would be lost forever,
had Jesus not hastened to help us.

Turning Point

In the ninth book of his *Confessions,*
Saint Augustine describes a moving episode.
He and his mother were standing at a window
overlooking the garden of their villa.

They had come to the villa from the city
to get away from the noisy crowds
and to get some much-needed rest.
Augustine writes:

And so the two of us, all alone,
were enjoying a very pleasant conversation,
"forgetting the past
and pushing on to what is ahead."
We were asking one another
in the presence of Truth—
what it would be like to share
the eternal life enjoyed by the saints. . . .

In the course of our conversation that day,
the world and its pleasures
lost all their attraction for us.

That episode was an important turning point
in the conversion and life of Augustine.

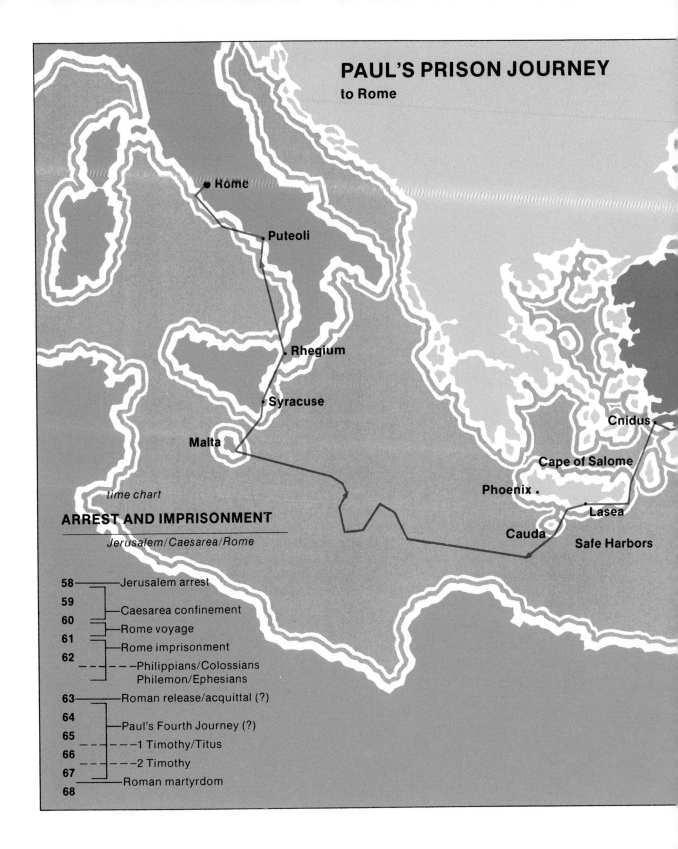

PAUL'S PRISON JOURNEY
to Rome

Rome

Puteoli

. Rhegium

. Syracuse

Malta

Cnidus .

Cape of Salome

Phoenix .

Lasea

Cauda

Safe Harbors

time chart

ARREST AND IMPRISONMENT

Jerusalem/Caesarea/Rome

58 — Jerusalem arrest
59 — Caesarea confinement
60 — Rome voyage
61 — Rome imprisonment
62 — — — — Philippians/Colossians
        Philemon/Ephesians
63 — Roman release/acquittal (?)
64 — Paul's Fourth Journey (?)
65 — — — — 1 Timothy/Titus
66 — — — — 2 Timothy
67 — Roman martyrdom
68

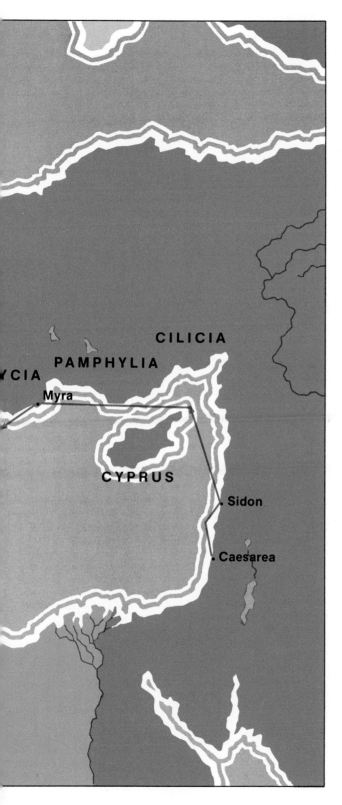

PART SIX

PRISON AND ROME

Acts 23-28

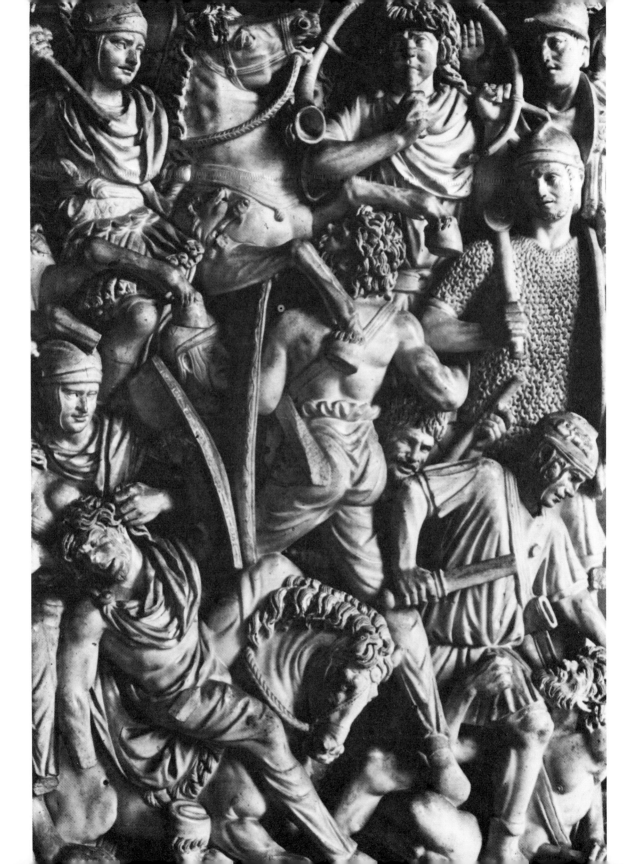

These Roman soldiers
are attacking enemy barbarians.
Their battle attire and weapons
are probably quite similar to
those used by the Roman soldiers
who rescued Paul in the temple area.

23

Council Confrontation

The air was crackling with tension
when Paul stood before the Jewish Council
the next day.

*Paul looked straight at the Council
and said, "My fellow Israelites!
My conscience is perfectly clear
about the way in which I have lived
before God to this very day."
The High Priest Ananias
ordered those who were standing close to Paul
to strike him on the mouth.
Paul said to him,
"God will certainly strike you—
you whitewashed wall!
You sit there
to judge me according to the Law,
yet you break the Law
by ordering them to strike me!"*

*The men close to Paul said to him,
"You are insulting God's High Priest!"*

*Paul answered,
"My fellow Israelites,
I did not know that he was the High Priest."*

ACTS 23:1-5

The order to strike Paul seems incredible
before such a respected group.
But it does fit the ugly portrait of Ananias,
painted in Josephus's *Jewish Antiquities* (20, 9:1-2).

It is not clear what Paul meant when he said
he did not know Ananias was the high priest.
He might have been inferring
that Ananias was unworthy of such an office.

DIVIDING THE COUNCIL

Then Paul took a calculated risk
in a desperate effort to defend himself.
He accused the Sadducees on the Council
of opposing him because of his belief in
and preaching of the resurrection.

*As soon as he said this, the Pharisees
and Sadducees started to quarrel,
and the group was divided. (For the Sadducees
say that people will not rise from death. . . .)
The shouting . . . became so violent
that the commander . . . ordered his soldiers
to go down into the group, get Paul away
from them, and take him into the fort.*

ACTS 23:7-10

145

When night fell, Paul found himself,
for a second time, in Roman custody.
As he sat there in the darkness of the jail,
his mind, perhaps, replayed recent events.

Paul must have asked himself
if his preaching efforts for Jesus would end,
as did the efforts of John the Baptist,
in death (Mark 6:14-29).

Then something strange happened.
Paul experienced the Lord's assurance.

"Don't be afraid!
You have given your witness for me here
in Jerusalem,
and you must also do the same in Rome."

ACTS 23:11

That night Paul slept soundly.

DEATH PLOT

But while Paul slept soundly,
his enemies were burning midnight oil.
Angered that neither the temple riot
nor the Council had solved their problem,
they decided to use their own methods.

They took a vow
that they would not eat or drink anything
until they had killed Paul.
There were more than forty
who planned this together....

But the son of Paul's sister
heard about the plot;
so he went to the fort and told Paul.

ACTS 23:12-13, 16

Paul, in turn, alerted the commander.
The commander didn't waste a minute.
He organized an armed guard
to escort Paul to Caesarea.

Paul would be safe in Caesarea.
Located about 60 miles northwest of Jerusalem,
it was the official residence
of the Roman governors of Palestine.

LETTER OF EXPLANATION

Then the commander
wrote a letter that went like this:

"Claudius Lysias
to His Excellency, Governor Felix: Greetings.

"The Jews seized this man
and were about to kill him.
I learned that he is a Roman citizen,
so I went with my soldiers and rescued him.
I wanted to know what they were accusing him of,
so I took him down to their Council.
I found out that he had not done a thing
for which he deserved to die or be put in prison;
the accusation against him
had to do with questions about their own law.
And when I was informed
that there was a plot against him,
at once I decided to send him to you.
I have told his accusers to make their charges
against him before you."

ACTS 23:25-30

The armed guard left quietly with Paul,
under cover of darkness.
They arrived at Caesarea without incident.

The governor read the letter
and asked Paul what province he was from.
When he found out
that he was from Cilicia, he said,
"I will hear you when your accusers arrive."
Then he gave orders
for Paul to be kept under guard
in the governor's headquarters.

ACTS 23:34-35

GOVERNOR FELIX

The story of Marcus Antonius Felix
sounds like the work of a movie scriptwriter.
Born a slave,
he caught the eye of the emperor Claudius,
who made him a freedman.

Felix went on to marry the granddaughter
of Mark Antony and Cleopatra
and become the first slave in Roman history
to be appointed a provincial governor.

Ruling Palestine from A.D. 52 to 57,
Felix proved totally insensitive to the Jews.
In fact, many historians lay at his doorstep
the permanent rebellion of Jews from Rome
which climaxed in the war of A.D. 66-70.

The Life of Paul
BENJAMIN WILLARD ROBINSON

Tacitus says that even when ruling a province
he did it "in the spirit of a slave."
He was one of the least efficient governors
of Judea.
He accepted bribes
wherever and whenever he could get them.
When he found the Jews restless
he deliberately took advantage of the situation
by fomenting uprisings
that he might execute whom he wished
and confiscate their property for his own use.

This man was to hear Paul's case.

24
Caesarea Confinement

Five days after Paul's Caesarea confinement,
a delegation of accusers came from Jerusalem.
It included the high priest, some elders,
and a lawyer named Tertullus.

Felix arranged an immediate hearing.
When all was ready,
Paul was summoned to the hearing room.
Tertullus stood up and began:

"Your Excellency!
Your wise leadership has brought us
a long period of peace,
and many necessary reforms are being made
for the good of our country.
We welcome this everywhere and at all times,
and we are deeply grateful to you.
I do not want to take up
too much of your time, however,
so I beg you to be kind and listen to
our brief account.
We found this man to be a dangerous nuisance;
he starts riots among the Jews all over the world
and is a leader of the party of the Nazarenes.
He also tried to defile the Temple,
and we arrested him.

147

If you question this man,
you yourself will be able to learn from him
all the things that we are accusing him of."

ACTS 24:2-8

Tertullus's introductory remarks
were calculated to win the favor of Felix.
Similarly, Tertullus's charges
were calculated to stir the concern of Felix.

First, he accused Paul of triggering riots,
not only in Jerusalem but outside it.
Romans tolerated many things,
but civil disorder was not one of them.

Second, Tertullus accused Paul
of leadership of a party
founded by one who was executed as a criminal.
If the tree's "root" was diseased,
how could its "sprouts" be free from disease?

Finally, he accused Paul of defiling the temple.
The Romans treated the temple with respect.
They would not tolerate someone
who flaunted it.

PAUL'S DEFENSE

When Tertullus concluded his remarks,
Felix turned to Paul for a response.
Paul began:

"I am happy to defend myself before you.
As you can find out for yourself,
it was no more than twelve days ago
that I went to Jerusalem to worship.
The Jews did not find me
arguing with anyone in the Temple,
nor did they find me stirring up the people,
either in the synagogues
or anywhere else in the city.
Nor can they give you proof of the accusations
they now bring against me.
I do admit this to you:
I worship the God of our ancestors
by following that Way which they say is false.
But I also believe
in everything written in the Law of Moses
and the books of the prophets."

ACTS 24:10-14

Paul was confined inland from these ancient harbor ruins.
A vivid picture of Caesarea is preserved
in Josephus's *Antiquities*.

"Always free from sea waves," it was protected
by a great breakwater on top of which were built
stone lodgings for visiting seafarers.

Next, Paul addressed himself to the charge
that he had defiled the temple.
He issued a challenge
to those who made this claim against him.

"They themselves ought to come before you
and make their accusations
if they have anything against me."

ACTS 24:19

Then he pointed to the Jerusalem delegation
and said:

"Or let these men here
tell what crime they found me guilty of
when I stood before the Council—
except for the one thing I called out
when I stood before them:
'I am being tried by you today for believing
that the dead will rise to life.'"

Then Felix,
who was well informed about the Way,
brought the hearing to a close.
"When the commander Lysias arrives,"
he told them, "I will decide your case."

ACTS 24:20-22

With that, Felix dismissed the delegation
and ordered Paul to be kept under guard.

AFTERMATH

A few days later,
Felix and his third wife, Drusilla,
the Jewish daughter of Herod Agrippa I,
sent for Paul to talk with him about the Way.

He . . . listened to [Paul]
as he talked about faith in Christ Jesus.
But as Paul went on discussing
about goodness, self-control,
and the coming Day of Judgment,

Felix was afraid and said, "You may leave now.
I will call you again when I get the chance."

ACTS 24:24-25

Felix's interest in Paul recalls
Herod Antipas's fascination with the Baptist.
Herod liked to talk with John,
"even though he became greatly disturbed
every time he heard him" (Mark 6:20).

John also pressed Herod on his illicit union
with Herodias (Mark 6:18),
just as Paul seems to have pressed Felix
on his illicit union with Drusilla.

But Felix had other motives as well.
He was hoping Paul would "buy" his release.
Luke says bluntly:

At the same time [Felix] was hoping
that Paul would give him some money;
and for this reason he would
call for him often and talk with him.

ACTS 24:26

When Paul refused "to go along,"
Felix held on to him for other motives:
"to gain favor with the Jews" (Acts 24:27).

Felix's game went on for two long years,
until Festus succeeded him as governor.
During this time, the great heart of Paul
cried out for freedom to preach the Gospel
to the millions of people beyond Caesarea.
But Paul had to be content with dreaming—
and praying.

25
Festus
Fiasco

Dietrich Bonhoeffer,
a German Lutheran pastor and theologian,
openly opposed the Nazis in World War II.
Eventually they seized him.
Like Paul, he spent two years in prison.
On April 9, 1945, he was executed.

Like Paul, Bonhoeffer wrote while in prison.
These random excerpts from his poem
"Night Voices"
preserve some of his prison thoughts.

Stretched out on my cot
I stare at the gray wall.
Outside, a summer evening
That does not know me
Goes singing into the countryside. . . .

Night and silence. . . .
I hear my own soul tremble and heave. . . .
I hear the uneasy creak of the beds. . . .
I hear how sleepless men toss and turn,
Who long for freedom. . . .

Night and silence. . . .

Suddenly I sat up,
As if, from a sinking ship, I had sighted land. . . .
But wherever I look, grasp, or seize,
There is only the impenetrable mass of darkness. . . .

Brother, till the night be past,
Pray for me!

DASHED HOPES

Paul experienced the long nights like this, too.
Then one day his hopes soared briefly.
Festus replaced Felix as Roman governor.

But as quickly as Paul's hopes soared,
they crashed.
It soon became clear that Paul's adversaries
were laying plans to exploit Festus's inexperience.

Shortly after Festus took over his new office,
he visited Jerusalem.
Paul's opponents were waiting for him.

While a prisoner in Caesarea,
Paul drank water that may have flowed
down this aqueduct.
Its origin was the Carmel hills 20 miles away,
from which it sloped an average of 12 inches
every 200 feet.
This facilitated the flow of water
through pipelike channels.

They begged Festus to do them the favor
of having Paul come to Jerusalem,
for they had made a plot
to kill him on the way.
Festus answered,
"Paul is being kept a prisoner in Caesarea,
and I myself will be going back there soon.
Let your leaders go to Caesarea with me
and accuse the man
if he has done anything wrong."

ACTS 25:2-5

THE HEARING

Two weeks later,
Paul's adversaries arrived in Caesarea.
The hearing before Festus was almost a replay
of the one two years earlier.

But Festus
wanted to gain favor with the Jews,
so he asked Paul,
"Would you be willing to go to Jerusalem
and be tried on these charges . . .?"

ACTS 25:9

Paul saw the danger immediately.
He did the only thing he could.
He appealed to the emperor.

Every Roman citizen had the right
to appeal his case to the emperor.
A law from Octavian's time
stated that if a citizen living outside Rome
had misgivings
about getting justice in a provincial court,
he could have his case heard in Rome.
Only a citizen caught in the act of violence
was denied appeal.

Festus seemed relieved at Paul's appeal.
It got him off the hook with Jewish leaders.

151

AGRIPPA II

Some time later
King Agrippa and Bernice came to Caesarea
to pay a visit of welcome to Festus.

ACTS 25:13

26
Agrippa
Audience

King Agrippa II
was the great-grandson of Herod the Great.
At 17, upon his father's death,
he was appointed king of northern Palestine.
Agrippa's visit gave Festus a chance
to confer with the king about Paul's case.

"There is a man here
who was left a prisoner by Felix;
and when I went to Jerusalem,
the Jewish chief priests and elders
brought charges against him
and asked me to condemn him. . . .
All they had were some arguments with him
about their own religion
and about a man named Jesus, who has died;
but Paul claims that he is alive. . . .
So I asked Paul if he would be willing
to go to Jerusalem and be tried. . . .
But Paul appealed . . .
to let the Emperor decide his case. . . .

"But I have nothing definite about him
to write to the Emperor."

ACTS 25:14–15, 19–21, 26

Agrippa took an immediate interest
in the case and asked to meet with Paul.
A meeting was arranged for the next day.

The next day Agrippa and Bernice
came with great pomp and ceremony
and entered the audience hall
with the military chiefs
and the leading men of the city.
Festus gave the order, and Paul was brought in.

ACTS 25:23

A hush fell upon the assembly
when Paul appeared in chains.
His prison garb contrasted dramatically
with the splendor and elegance of the court.

But Paul's appearance,
judging from what followed,
must have radiated a profound power.

When the proper formalities were honored,
Festus turned the meeting over to Agrippa,
who gave Paul permission to speak.

Paul stretched out his hand. . . .

"King Agrippa! . . .

"All the Jews know how I have lived . . .
as a member of the strictest party
of our religion, the Pharisees. . . .

152

"I myself thought
that I should do everything I could
against the cause of Jesus of Nazareth. . . .

"It was for this purpose
that I went to Damascus with authority
and orders from the chief priests.
It was on the road at midday,
Your Majesty, that I saw a light
much brighter than the sun,
coming from the sky
and shining around me. . . .
'Who are you, Lord?' I asked.
And the Lord answered,
'I am Jesus, whom you persecute.
But get up and stand on your feet.
I have appeared to you
to appoint you as my servant.
You are to tell others
what you have seen of me today
and what I will show you in the future. . . .
You are to open their eyes
and turn them from the darkness
to the light. . . .'

"And so, King Agrippa,
I did not disobey the vision. . . .
It was for this reason that the Jews
seized me while I was in the Temple,
and they tried to kill me. . . .
What I say
is the very same thing which the prophets
and Moses said was going to happen:
that the Messiah must suffer
and be the first one to rise from death,
to announce the light of salvation
to the Jews and to the Gentiles."

As Paul defended himself in this way,
Festus shouted at him, "You are mad, Paul!
Your great learning is driving you mad!"

ACTS 26:1–24

Saying "Yes"

One of the most decorated U.S. chaplains,
William McCorkle,
resisted the call of God for a long time.
Finally he saw the futility of fighting God.
He sat down and wrote in his Bible:

Tonight I give in;
I'll do whatever you want me to do.

From that day forward
his life took on new purpose and meaning.

Paul's conversion on the road to Damascus
seems to have fit a similar pattern.
God said to Paul:

You are hurting yourself by hitting back,
like an ox kicking against its owner's stick.

This Greek proverb
was used by Euripides in one of his plays
to show the uselessness of struggling
against one's destiny.

Once Paul realized the truth about Jesus
and the destiny to which he was being called,
Paul said yes to both.
From that moment forward,
his life took on new purpose and meaning.

Agrippa became king in A.D. 50
and stayed loyal to Rome
during the Jewish Revolt (A.D. 67–70).

Shortly before his death (ca. A.D. 100),
Agrippa minted a bronze coin (above)
showing Emperor Domitian on the front
and Tyche (goddess of fortune) on the back,
holding barley stalks and a horn of plenty.

The bronze coin of Vespasian (below)
commemorates the end of the Jewish Revolt
(JUDAEA CAPTA, "Judea Captured").
A palm tree, symbol of Israel,
and a seated, mourning Jewess
complete the motif.

Then Paul paused dramatically.
Looking straight at King Agrippa, he said:

"King Agrippa!
I can speak to you with all boldness,
because you know about these things.
I am sure that you have taken notice
of every one of them,
for this thing has not happened
hidden away in a corner.
King Agrippa, do you believe the prophets?
I know that you do!"

ACTS 26:26–27

The king was amazed and charmed
at Paul's candor and boldness.
Fully poised, yet somewhat moved, he said to Paul:

"In this short time
do you think you will make me a Christian?"

"Whether a short time or a long time,"
Paul answered, "my prayer to God is
that you and all the rest of you
who are listening to me today
might become what I am—
except, of course, for these chains!"

ACTS 26:28–29

With this sincere prayer
and gentle touch of humor,
Paul bowed to the assembly and stepped aside.

Then the king, the governor, Bernice,
and all the others got up,
and after leaving they said to each other,
"This man has not done anything
for which he should die or be put in prison."
And Agrippa said to Festus,
"This man could have been released
if he had not appealed to the Emperor."

ACTS 26:30–32

27

Voyage and Shipwreck

On January 17, 1912,
five explorers leaped and shouted for joy
as they reached the South Pole.
It was a remarkable human achievement.

But their exciting victory turned to ashes
during their 800-mile return to civilization.
Two explorers met death along the way.
The three remaining explorers
collapsed just 11 miles short of safety.

When the bodies were found,
the papers and journals of the explorers
were still intact and readable.
An excerpt from the journal of Edward Wilson
sounds like something Paul might have written
as he set out from Caesarea for Rome.

The Faith of Edward Wilson
GEORGE SEAVER

"So I live, knowing that I am in God's hands,
to be used to bring others to Him . . .
or to die tomorrow if He so wills. . . .
We must do what we can
and leave the rest to Him. . . .
My trust is in God,
so that it matters not what I do or where I go."

JOURNEY TO ROME

Just as Wilson
kept a journal of his polar expedition,
so Luke appears to have kept a journal
of Paul's sea voyage to Rome.

The description of this trip in Acts,
written in the first person, is remarkably detailed.
It is unique among ancient writings
for describing the hazards of sea voyages
before compasses and sextants existed.

Paul was just one of many other prisoners
being transported under a military guard,
commanded by an officer named Julius.
Who were these "other" prisoners?

St. Paul the Traveller
and the Roman Citizen
WILLIAM M. RAMSAY

The others had been in all probability
already condemned to death,
and were going to supply the perpetual demand
which Rome made on the provinces
for human victims to amuse the populace
by their death in the arena.

Making the trip with Paul
were Luke and Aristarchus (Acts 19:29).
They probably signed on the passenger list
as Paul's personal servants.

Citing an ancient letter of Pliny,
Sir William Ramsay notes that Roman citizens
had the right to servants, even in custody.

SIDON

The first stop on the voyage was at Sidon,
a port 47 miles up the coast from Caesarea.
Here there was a Christian community,
possibly dating from Jesus' day (Luke 6:17).

"We kept close to the coast and
with great difficulty
came to a place called Safe Harbors,
not far from the town of Lasea
[on the island of Crete]."

Acts 27:8

Paul seems to have enjoyed Julius's respect,
for Luke tells us:

Julius was kind to Paul
and allowed him to go and see his friends,
to be given what he needed.

ACTS 27:3

MYRA

From Sidon, the ship set its sails for Myra.
Luke writes:

Because the winds were blowing against us,
we sailed on the sheltered side
of the island of Cyprus.

We crossed over the sea . . . to Myra in Lycia.
There the officer found a ship
from Alexandria that was going to sail for Italy,
so he put us aboard.

ACTS 27:4–6

Ships loaded with grain
traveled regularly from Egypt to Italy.
No doubt the ship was carrying produce
to Roman markets.

We sailed slowly for several days
and with great difficulty
finally arrived off the town of Cnidus.

ACTS 27:7

The harbor
was not a good one to spend the winter in;
so most of the men
were in favor of putting out to sea
and trying to reach Phoenix . . .
a harbor in Crete
that faces southwest and northwest.

ACTS 27:9, 12

The Day of Atonement
fell in late September or early October.
Sailing after this date was hazardous
because of the turbulent winter weather.

SAFE HARBORS

Bad wind conditions
then forced the ship to sail down to Crete,
where it tacked along the sheltered coast
until it reached Safe Harbors.

We spent a long time there,
until it became dangerous
to continue the voyage, for by now
the Day of Atonement was already past. . . .

But a "soft wind from the south" was blowing,
so the captain decided to take a gamble.
He made the wrong decision.
Soon a violent storm blew up.

Since it was impossible
to keep the ship headed into the wind,
we gave up trying
and let it be carried along by the wind. . . .

156

Painted Eyes

Ancient ships were remarkable.
Lengths of 100-150 feet were ordinary.
Usually they had a single mast
with a huge single sail of linen or hides.
This made steering awkward at best.
Ancient ships were also colorful.

Ambassador for Christ
WILLIAM BARCLAY

The stern was brought up
and bent round like a goose's neck.
Usually at the prow
they had two great eyes painted,
as if the ship had to see her way across the sea.
Often they were called after some god
whose image was at the front of the prow
like a figurehead.
They had no hinged rudder as our ships have,
but were steered with two great paddles
coming out, one from each side,
from the hull near the stern.

Most ancient ships carried dinghies (Acts 27:30).
They were towed astern in good weather
but hauled aboard in storms.
The reason for carrying the dinghy
was not for emergency use but for harbor use.

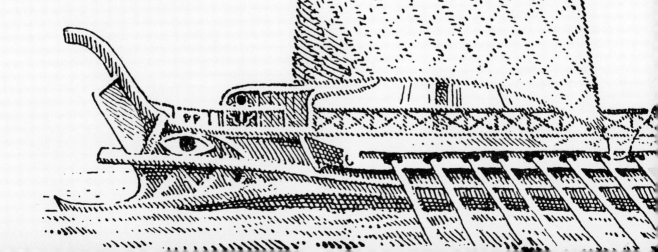

The violent storm continued,
so on the next day they began to throw
some of the ship's cargo overboard. . . .
For many days
we could not see the sun or the stars,
and the wind kept on blowing very hard.
We finally gave up all hope of being saved.

ACTS 27:15, 18-20

It was in this situation
that Paul gave the crew renewed hope.

"Men, . . . take courage! . . .
For last night
an angel of the God to whom I belong
and whom I worship came to me and said,
'Don't be afraid, Paul!
You must stand before the Emperor.
And God in his goodness to you
has spared the lives
of all those who are sailing with you.'"

ACTS 27:21-24

When day came,
the sailors did not recognize the coast,
but they noticed a bay with a beach
and decided that, if possible,
they would run the ship aground there. . . .
But the ship hit a sandbank . . . ;
the front part . . . could not move,
while the back part was being broken to pieces
by the violence of the waves.

The soldiers made a plan to kill all the prisoners,
in order to keep them from swimming ashore
and escaping.
But the army officer wanted to save Paul,
so he stopped them. . . .
He ordered all the men who could swim
to jump overboard first and swim ashore;
the rest were to follow,
holding on to the planks
or to some broken pieces of the ship.
And this was how we all got safely ashore.

ACTS 27:33-44

THE WRECK

For two weeks
the helpless ship was carried like a cork
across 300 miles of wild, seething sea.
Then one night the crew realized
that the ship was in shallow waters.
They were thrown into a state of panic,
fearing the ship would "go on the rocks."
Somehow the crew survived the night.

Just before dawn . . . Paul took some bread,
gave thanks to God before them all,
broke it, and began to eat.
They took courage,
and every one of them also ate some food. . . .
After everyone had eaten enough,
they lightened the ship
by throwing all the wheat into the sea.

Standing on these cliffs,
the island dwellers of Malta watched survivors
swim ashore from the shipwreck.
Appropriately, the word *Malta* derives its name
from the Phoenician word meaning "refuge."
The bay, shown in the foreground,
still bears the name "St. Paul's Bay."

158

28
Rescue and Rome

Half-naked sailors swimming vigorously,
armed soldiers dog-paddling behind planks,
prisoners clinging to wreckage—
this was the amazing sight
that greeted the island dwellers of Malta
as they ran excitedly to the beach.
Describing what then followed, Luke says:

The natives there were very friendly to us.
It had started to rain and was cold,
so they built a fire and made us all welcome.

Paul gathered up a bundle of sticks
and was putting them on the fire
when a snake came out on account of the heat
and fastened itself to his hand.
The natives saw the snake hanging
on Paul's hand and said to one another,
"This man must be a murderer,
but Fate will not let him live,
even though he escaped from the sea."
But Paul shook the snake off into the fire
without being harmed at all.
They were waiting for him to swell up
or suddenly fall down dead.
But after waiting for a long time
and not seeing anything unusual happening
to him, they changed their minds and said,
"He is a god!"

ACTS 28:2-6

The shipwrecked crew
was fortunate to land on friendly Malta.
There were other shores
where they would have been attacked—
even killed.

Eyes and Hands

This painting by El Greco invites questions
about Paul's personal appearance.
Two of Paul's traits
seem to have impressed Luke, in a special way.

St. Paul the Traveller
and the Roman Citizen
WILLIAM M. RAMSAY

*As an orator, he evidently used
a good deal of gesture with his hands;
for example,
he enforced a point to the Ephesian Elders
by showing them "these hands" (Acts 20:34).*

Paul's hand gestures are mentioned, also,
in his speech at Pisidian Antioch (Acts 13:16),
before the Jerusalem mob (Acts 21:40),
and before King Agrippa (Acts 26:1).

The second trait that seems to have
impressed Luke is Paul's eyes. Ramsay says:

*Two of the most remarkable instances
of Paul's power over others are prefaced
by the statement that Paul "fixed his eyes on"
the man (Acts 13:9, 14:9) . . .
and this suggests that his fixed, steady gaze
was a marked feature in his personality.*

The snake episode illustrates
the superstitious nature of the islanders.
It also brought Paul to the attention of
the "chief of the island," Publius (Acts 28:7).
The discovery of two ancient inscriptions
confirms the correctness of this title
and testifies to Luke's reliable reporting.

TO ROME

After three months,
spring arrived and sea travel resumed.
The shipwrecked crew booked passage
on a ship called "The Twin Gods" (Acts 28:11).
The twins, Castor and Pollux,
were favorite protectors of sailors.

From Malta, "The Twin Gods"
sailed to Syracuse, Rhegium, and Puteoli,
the ancient port of entry for Rome.

As the ship glided into Puteoli Bay,
Paul may have pointed an inquiring finger
at Mount Vesuvius in the distance.
Framed beautifully against the blue sky,
it gave no sign
that the fatal countdown for its explosion
was already in progress.

Ironically, points out Josephus,
Drusilla, whose husband, Felix,
denied Paul's plea for freedom in Caesarea,
was destined to visit Pompeii and be killed
by volcanic ash erupting from Mount Vesuvius.

The Journeys of St. Paul
STEWART PEROWNE

*Much of Roman Puteoli is now,
owing to seismic displacement, under the water,
but enough remains,*

including a great brick amphitheater
(later than Paul's day),
to suggest to us what a thriving, busy,
bawdy harbour it must have been. . . .
No doubt the arrival of the ship
had caused quite a sensation.
Seneca tells . . .
how the population of the town
rushed down to the quays
when an Egyptian grain ship was sighted.

After a brief stay in Puteoli,
Paul headed north for Rome, 130 miles away.
The Appian Way—the "queen" of the roads,
which he followed—still exists today.
Scars from countless ancient wheels furrow it
like wrinkles on a tired face.
Luke writes about the journey to Rome:

The believers in Rome heard about us
and came as far as the towns of
Market of Appius and Three Inns to meet us.
When Paul saw them,
he thanked God and was greatly encouraged.

When we arrived in Rome,
Paul was allowed to live by himself
with a soldier guarding him.

ACTS 28:15-16

In other words,
Paul was put under a form of house arrest.

PAUL'S ROME

The Rome that Paul entered was magnificent.
Yet there were many things about it
that were shocking.

Perowne notes that one of them was
the total absence of sanitation.
Dung heaps and cesspools lay at intervals,
and human refuse was carried to them.

Unfortunately, however, many people
simply threw the refuse into the streets.

Similarly, the noise in Rome was appalling.
Seneca writes that he found it unbearable.
By day, roving priests of Isis and Cybele
chanted their exotic cantations
to the rhythmic beat of clashing cymbals.
At night, heavy wagons
clanked over cobblestone streets,
waking everyone within earshot.

It was to this city
that Paul brought the message of Jesus
and began to preach it uncompromisingly.
Paul wasted no time. Luke writes:

After three days Paul called
the local Jewish leaders to a meeting. . . .

They said to him,
"We have not received any letters from Judea
about you, nor have any of our people
come from there with any news
or anything bad to say about you.
But we would like to hear your ideas,
because we know that everywhere
people speak against this party
to which you belong."

ACTS 28:17, 21-22

Paul was delighted with the opportunity
to talk about Jesus.

From morning till night
he explained to them his message
about the Kingdom of God,
and he tried to convince them about Jesus
by quoting from the Law of Moses
and the writings of the prophets.
Some of them were convinced by his words,
but others would not believe.

ACTS 28:23-24

Paul warned the cynics,
using the blunt words of Isaiah the prophet,

"'Go and say to this people:
You will listen and listen, but not understand;
you will look and look, but not see. . . .'"

For two years
Paul lived in a place he rented for himself,
and there he welcomed all who came to see him.
He preached about the Kingdom of God
and taught about the Lord Jesus Christ,
speaking with all boldness and freedom.

ACTS 28:26, 30-31

UNFINISHED STORY

What eventually happened to Paul?
Acts does not say.
The pastoral letters, however,
suggest that he was freed after a first trial
(2 Timothy 4:16).
Possibly, then, he went to Spain (Romans 15:24),
and to Asia Minor (Titus 3:12), Macedonia
(1 Timothy 1:3), and Crete (Titus 1:5).

Once back in Rome,
Paul was brought to trial a second time
and convicted (2 Timothy 4:6, 16).
Finally, outside Rome, around A.D. 67,
he was beheaded.
Tradition says
the church of St. Paul-Outside-the-Walls
marks his burial place.

One last question:
Why did Luke leave Acts unfinished?
Of all the theories,
perhaps the most satisfying one is this:
Luke left Acts unfinished
because the story of Acts is still unfinished.
The preaching of the Good News
goes on—and must go on—
until Jesus returns in final glory.

"When I have finished this task . . .
I shall leave for Spain."

Romans 15:28

Paul may have visited here.

Augustus Caesar's upraised arm
toward the tower walls of Terraco, Spain
(modern Tarragona), recalls the seaport's
important place in Roman history.

162

Prison Letters

All the boards are rotten.
On the ground filth lies an inch thick....
We are packed like herrings in a barrel....
From twilight till morning we are forbidden
to leave the barrack-room;
the doors are barricaded;
in the ante-room a great wooden trough
for the calls of nature is placed;
this makes one almost unable to breathe.
All the prisoners stink like pigs;
they say that they can't help it.

This is how the famous Russian author
Feodor Dostoevski described conditions
during his four-year confinement
as a political prisoner in Siberia.

Paul was not imprisoned in Rome
under such wretched conditions.
His imprisonment was nonetheless restricting
and humiliating.

Paul used his time in prison to preach,
not only by word of mouth
but also by letter.
The prison letters include:

Philippians (1:7)   Philemon (23)
Colossians (4:10)   Ephesians (6:20)

Tradition says these letters were written
during Paul's Rome imprisonment,
but not all scholars agree.

It is not always easy to say
when or where Paul wrote his letters.
For example, his Letter to the Philippians
was penned in prison (1:7).
But was it Ephesus (early 50s),
Caesarea (late 50s), or Rome (early/late 60s)?

Some evidence suggesting that it was Rome
is reference to the "palace guard" (1:13)
and persons in the "Emperor's palace" (4:22).
Some evidence suggesting that it was Ephesus
is the presence of an early preaching theme:
"The Lord is coming soon" (4:5).

The important point, however, is *not*
the prison from which the letter was written
but the teaching it preserves.

PHILIPPIANS

Mark Twain's story
entitled "The Terrible Catastrophe"
concerns a group of people so entrapped
they can do nothing to save themselves.
The famous humorist ends his story by saying:
"I have these characters in such a fix
that I cannot get them out.
Anyone who thinks he can is welcome to try."

Although Mark Twain never intended it,
his story is a perfect parable
of the world situation before Jesus' birth.

Several Letters?

An interesting passage
appears in a second-century letter
from Bishop Polycarp to the church at Philippi.
After recalling how Paul preached there,
the bishop notes:

When he was absent, he wrote you letters.
By carefully studying these letters,
you can strengthen yourself
in the faith that has been given you.

Polycarp speaks of "letters,"
but we have only one letter to the Philippians.
Some scholars suggest that this one letter
might be the result
of combining and editing three letters.

One letter (1:3-3:1)
addresses two problems among the Philippians:
internal disunity (1:15-18)
and external persecution (1:28-29).
It appears to end: "In conclusion" (3:1).

Another letter begins: "I don't mind repeating
what I have written before" (3:1).
This letter warns the Philippians
against Judaizers who insist that Christians
must be circumcised (3:2-6).
It appears to end: "In conclusion" (4:8).

Finally, the third letter (4:10-20)
seems to be a simple note of thanksgiving.
It ends: "To our God and Father be the glory
forever and ever! Amen."

Whether the letter to the Philippians
is one document or several
will probably be debated for years to come.
The outcome of the debate
cannot affect the letter's inspired status.

It was an ugly world.
Men and women were degraded
and sold for others' amusement
Oppression and exploitation were common.
Poverty, hatred, and sorrow
hung like clouds over every town and city.

It is no accident, therefore,
that the angel said to Joseph about the infant:
"You will name him Jesus—
because he will save his people
from their sins" (Matthew 1:21).
Describing Jesus, Paul wrote the Philippians:

He always had the nature of God,
but he did not think that by force
he should try to become equal with God.
Instead of this,
of his own free will he gave up all he had,
and took the nature of a servant.
He became like man
and appeared in human likeness.
He was humble
and walked the path of obedience
all the way to death—his death on the cross.

For this reason God raised him
to the highest place above
and gave him the name
that is greater than any other name.
And so, in honor of the name of Jesus
all beings in heaven,
on earth, and in the world below
will fall on their knees,
and all will openly proclaim
that Jesus Christ is Lord,
to the glory of God the Father.

PHILIPPIANS 2:6-11

This "meditation" on Jesus
flows so rhythmically in the original Greek
that some think it was a poetic hymn.

Exhorting the Philippians to imitate Jesus
in dealing with pagan neighbors, Paul says:
"You must shine among them
like stars lighting up the sky."

Philippians 2:15

Lamplighter

One night, when he was old,
John Ruskin, the 19th-century British writer,
was sitting in front of a window in his home.
He was staring out into the night
across town to a distant hillside street.
There, the flaming torch of the town lamplighter
was igniting streetlamp after streetlamp.
Because of the darkness,
you could not see the lamplighter himself.

All you could see was his torch
and the trail of lights he left behind him.

*After a few minutes
Ruskin turned to a friend and said,
"That illustrates
what I mean by a genuine Christian.
You may not know him or ever see him,
but his way has been marked
by the lights he leaves burning."*

Ralph L. Woods

Reminiscent of Isaiah 52:13 and 45:23,
it makes a beautiful creed
or summary of the Good News:

Jesus, the eternal Son of the eternal Father,
took flesh, suffered, died, rose, ascended,
and now reigns over all creation.

Whether Paul composed the hymn
or merely cited it,
he used it as the guiding star of his life.

All I want is to know Christ and to experience
the power of his resurrection,
to share in his sufferings
and become like him in his death, in the hope
that I myself will be raised from death to life.

PHILIPPIANS 3:10

Paul ends his letter with this exhortation:

Show a gentle attitude toward everyone.
The Lord is coming soon.
Don't worry about anything,
but in all your prayers
ask God for what you need,
always asking him with a thankful heart.
And God's peace,
which is far beyond human understanding,
will keep your hearts and minds safe
in union with Christ Jesus.

PHILIPPIANS 4:5-7

COLOSSIANS

In 1945, some Egyptian diggers
unearthed a sealed jar near Nag Hammadi.
At first they hesitated to break open the jar
for fear it contained a *jinn* ("spirit").
But the dream of a buried treasure
overcame the fear of the *jinn*.

The jar contained 13 Gnostic documents
dating from about the fourth century A.D.

Gnosticism derived its name
from the Greek word for "knowledge."
One teaching of Gnosticism was
that certain "spirits" controlled human affairs.
It also taught how to placate these "spirits."

Scholars believe Gnostics came to Colossae
and were upsetting Christian converts.
The Colossians were not taught by Paul
(Colossians 2:1),
but by Epaphras, who sought Paul's advice
on two questions, especially.

The first seems to have centered around
the control these spirits had over humans.
Paul responded not by entering into debate
about such spiritual rulers.
He simply affirmed that Christ "is supreme
over every spiritual ruler" (Colossians 2:10).
He affirmed this superiority beautifully
in what some believe to be an early creed.

Christ is the visible likeness
of the invisible God.
He is the first-born Son,
superior to all created things. . . .
Christ existed before all things,
and in union with him
all things have their proper place.
He is the head of his body, the church;
he is the source of the body's life.
He is the first-born Son,
who was raised from death,
in order that he alone might have
the first place in all things. . . .
God made peace
through his Son's . . . death on the cross
and so brought back to himself all things,
both on earth and in heaven.

COLOSSIANS 1:15-20

Epaphras's second question
dealt with certain external practices

Somebody Else's Mail?

A *Peanuts* cartoon
shows Charlie Brown and Linus
talking about the letters of Paul.
As the conversation unfolds,
Linus confesses to having guilt feelings
about reading Paul's letters, saying:
"I always feel like
I'm reading somebody else's mail."

Paul didn't mind having other people
read his letters.
He encouraged it, telling the Colossians:

After you read this letter,
make sure that it is read also
in the church at Laodicea.
At the same time, you are to read the letter
that the brothers in Laodicea will send you.

COLOSSIANS 4:16

Early churches circulated Paul's letters.
This is clear from ancient manuscripts
of Paul's Letter to the Ephesians.

Searching the Scriptures
JOHN J. DOUGHERTY

The oldest and best manuscripts—
for example, Papyrus 46 and Codex Vaticanus—
do not have the reading "at Ephesus" in 1:1.
The internal evidence of the letter itself
does not suggest the community of Ephesus.
It seems that the letter was a circular letter
addressed to several churches of Asia Minor
in the neighborhood of Ephesus,
and that a space was left blank
to be filled in
according to the place where it was read.

that were apparently linked to the "spirit cult."
Again, Paul avoided useless debate
and reminded the Colossian Christians:

You have died with Christ
and are set free
from the ruling spirits of the universe.
Why, then, do you . . . obey such rules
as "Don't handle this," "Don't taste that,"
"Don't touch the other"? . . .

You have been raised to life with Christ,
so set your hearts on the things
that are in heaven. . . .

Clothe yourself with compassion, kindness,
humility, gentleness, and patience. . . .

Forgive one another. . . .
And to all these qualities add love,
which binds all things together in perfect unity.

COLOSSIANS 2:20-21; 3:1, 12-14

Paul ends with some practical suggestions
for husband-wife, child-parent,
and slave-master relationships
(Colossians 3:18-4:1).
It is pointless
to apply modern standards to ancient times
for purposes of determining whether or not
Paul was a male chauvinist or pro-slaver.

Paul addressed the concrete situations
of his time and provided guidelines for them.

167

PHILEMON

"I have escaped, hold me.
If you return me to my owner [name]
you shall receive a *solidum* [gold coin]."

The hunk of metal
containing these words, inscribed in Latin,
is now displayed in a museum in Rome.
It once hung from a chain around a slave's neck.

The inscription
recalls one of Paul's most moving letters.
It concerns a runaway slave, Onesimus,
whom Paul befriended and baptized in Rome.

The letter is to a rich Colossian, Philemon,
also a new Christian, asking him
not only to forgive Onesimus
but also to receive him back as a brother.
Paul writes:

"I have escaped, hold me . . .
you shall receive a *solidum* [gold coin]"—
so says this 2¾" medal
that once hung from the neck
of an ancient Roman slave.

The Same Person?

A letter of Ignatius of Antioch
refers often to Onesimus, bishop of Ephesus.
Written around A.D. 110, the letter echoes
Paul's Letter to Philemon—even punning
on Onesimus's name, as Paul did.

*At one time, he [Onesimus—"useful," in Greek]
was of no use to you,
but now he is useful both to you and to me.*

PHILEMON 11

John Knox suggested that Bishop Onesimus
and the runaway slave were the same person.
(Onesimus, about 20 years old in Paul's time,
would have been about 70 in Ignatius's time.)

Knox's suggestion is especially fascinating
because scholars believe Paul's letters
were first gathered together and published
in Ephesus around Bishop Onesimus's time.

Who would have been interested in
and more qualified to direct this project
than the ex-slave who became a bishop?

168

I am sending him back to you now,
and with him goes my heart.
I would like to keep him here with me,
while I am in prison for the gospel's sake,
so that he could help me in your place.
However, I do not want to force you to help me;
rather, I would like for you to do it
of your own free will.
So I will not do anything unless you agree.

It may be that Onesimus was away from you
for a short time
so that you might have him back for all time.
And now he is not just a slave,
but much more than a slave:
he is a dear brother in Christ.
How much he means to me!
And how much more he will mean to you,
both as a slave and as a brother in the Lord!

So, if you think of me as your partner,
welcome him back just as you would welcome me.
If he has done you any wrong
or owes you anything, charge it to my account.
Here, I will write this with my own hand:
I, Paul, will pay you back.

PHILEMON 12-19

Paul concludes:

Epaphras, who is in prison with me
for the sake of Christ Jesus, sends you his greetings,
and so do my fellow workers Mark,
Aristarchus, Demas, and Luke.

May the grace of the Lord Jesus Christ
be with you all.

PHILEMON 23-25

The 25 short verses of this letter
illustrate beautifully Paul's earlier teachings
about the dignity of the Christian
and the love Christians should show
one another in their union in Christ.

EPHESIANS

"30 Years Later,
a Japanese Surrenders"
CHICAGO SUN-TIMES

Lubang Island, Philippines—
A World War II Japanese straggler
formally surrendered on this jungle island. . . .

Hiroo Onoda,
a former Japanese army lieutenant . . .
told Japanese newsmen
he had not come out before because
"I had not received the order." . . .

Japanese officials
have estimated that hundreds
if not thousands of World War II soldiers
could be hiding out
in the jungles of Southeast Asia—
either from ignorance of the war's end
or out of blind loyalty to a military code.

Thirty years after Jesus' resurrection
there were "stragglers" in Paul's world
who, either from ignorance or negligence,
were unaware that Jesus defeated Satan
and had begun a new world order.
The Letter to the Ephesians
(to borrow Karl Barth's insight)
shouted to such "stragglers."

"Wake up, sleeper, and rise from death,
and Christ will shine on you."

EPHESIANS 5:14

The Letter to the Ephesians is a
doctrinal summary and symphony of salvation
outlining God's grand plan for us.

God had already decided that through Jesus Christ
he would make us his sons—
this was his pleasure and purpose. . . .

Where Did They Meet?

Early Christians did not "go" to church,
because they thought of themselves
as "the church," the body of Christ
(Ephesians 1:23).

The first Christians met in private homes.
One of these was excavated in Dura-Europos
on the Euphrates River in the 1930s.

Biblical Archaeology
G. ERNEST WRIGHT

*In plan it consisted of a series of rooms
around a paved open court.
On a plastered wall was an inscription
stating when the house
was built, A.D. 232-3 in our calendar.
One of the rooms had been used as a chapel. . . .
In a small neighboring room was the baptistry.
At one end of it
was a niche and a receptacle or tub for the water.
Above the latter
a scene was painted on the wall,
showing Christ as the Good Shepherd. . . .
Other wall paintings show Scriptural scenes,
such as David and Goliath,
the Samaritan woman,
Peter attempting to walk on the water,
and the healing of the paralytic.*

"There is one Lord,
one faith, one baptism;
there is one God and Father
of all mankind."
Ephesians 4:5-6

*This plan, which God will complete
when the time is right,
is to bring all creation together,
everything in heaven and on earth,
with Christ as head. . . .*

*The church is Christ's body,
the completion of him
who himself completes all things everywhere.*

In the past you were spiritually dead. . . .
But God's mercy is so abundant,
and his love for us is so great,
that while we were spiritually dead . . .
he brought us to life with Christ. . . .
In our union with Christ Jesus
he raised us up with him
to rule with him in the heavenly world. . . .

Each one of us has received a special gift
in proportion to what Christ has given. . . .
He appointed some to be apostles,
others to be prophets,
others to be evangelists,
others to be pastors and teachers.
He did this to prepare all God's people
for the work of Christian service,
in order to build up the body of Christ. . . .
Under his control all the different parts
of the body fit together, and . . .
the whole body grows and builds itself up
through love. . . .

You yourselves used to be in the darkness,
but since you have become the Lord's people,
you are in the light.
So you must live like people
who belong to the light. . . .

At all times carry faith as a shield. . . .
And accept salvation as a helmet,
and the word of God as the sword
which the Spirit gives you.
Do all this in prayer, asking for God's help.
Pray on every occasion, as the Spirit leads.

EPHESIANS 1:5, 10, 23; 2:1-6; 4:7-16; 5:8; 6:16-18

Maverick Letter

"A stranger at the door"—that's how someone
described the Letter to the Ephesians
after comparing it with other Pauline letters.
What makes it a stranger?

First, its style is heavy compared to the others.

Second, its language is somewhat distinctive.
For example, 39 words in the letter
are not found elsewhere in the New Testament.

Third, its doctrine is more sophisticated.
Compared to Colossians, which it develops,
it represents a significant advance
(for example, church = the body of Christ).

These differences
have spawned an assortment of theories.
Some people even suggest that it was penned
by a later hand as a prologue or epilogue
to the completed collection of Paul's letters.
One writer sums up the theorizing this way:

Dictionary of the Bible
JOHN L. MCKENZIE

There are difficulties
both in attributing Ephesians to Paul
and in removing it from him. . . .
Actually Paul "wrote" no letters,
but dictated them in general terms.

Pastoral Letters

Careers of artists
frequently reflect "periods" of development.
When Chicago's Art Institute
acquired Pablo Picasso's *Girl with Pitcher*,
an art critic said:

"Art Institute's New 'Jewels'"
ALAN ARTNER

*"Girl with Pitcher". . . was painted
in the final year of his so-called Rose Period
and is one of its most beautiful highlights.
The artist
has assimilated various primitive influences
which were leading him closer
to the interpretation of landscapes, figures,
and still-lifes through geometric forms.*

"Periods" of development are evident, also,
in the preaching career of Paul.
This development is reflected in his letters.

The development appears to be so marked
in the pastoral letters
that many modern scholars suggest
that they were written by a disciple of Paul.

For example, the smooth, unrestrained style
of the pastoral letters contrasts sharply
with the rough, impassioned style
of Paul's earlier letters.
Similarly, their content reflects a developed
church structure (1 Timothy 3:1-3; 4:14; 5:22).

Dictionary of the Bible
JOHN L. MCKENZIE

These considerations
led many scholars of the 19th century
to place the Pastoral Epistles as late as A.D. 150.
This view is now abandoned;
they are quoted by Polycarp (155),
are very probably alluded to by Ignatius
of Antioch (107),
and are to be placed before 1 Clement (95),
which shows a more highly developed
hierarchical structure than the Pastoral Epistles.

Scholars, following a more traditional approach,
argue that the pastoral letters should be different,
because an older, more mature Paul
is handling dramatically different problems
in an older, more mature church.
But the debate continues,
and probably will continue for a long time.

I TIMOTHY

Paul and Timothy were close to each other.
This is evidenced by the fact
that Paul mentions him in almost all his letters.
Timothy was quite young (1 Timothy 4:12)
and was fragile in health (1 Timothy 5:23).
These things handicapped him somewhat
in his work.

173

"An athlete . . . cannot win the prize
unless he obeys the rules" (2 Timothy 2:5).
Popularity in sports was high in Paul's time.
This fifth-century B.C. athlete
was sculptured by the Greek artist Myron.

but anyway he said the key phrase was,
"Run to win.". . .
Vince has a knack for making all the saints
sound like they would have been
great football coaches.

Paul uses four "athletic images"
in his letters to Timothy.
Coach Lombardi's reference, however,
came from 1 Corinthians.

Surely you know
that many runners take part in a race,
but only one of them wins the prize.
Run, then, in such a way as to win the prize.
Every athlete in training
submits to strict discipline,
in order to be crowned with a wreath
that will not last;
but we do it for one that will last forever.
That is why I run straight for the finish line;
that is why I am like a boxer
who does not waste his punches.
I harden my body with blows
and bring it under complete control,
to keep myself from being disqualified
after having called others to the contest.

1 CORINTHIANS 9:24-27

The Athlete and Paul

Jerry Kramer, former Green Bay Packer all-pro,
wrote of a game with the Los Angeles Rams:

Instant Replay:
The Green Bay Diary of Jerry Kramer
EDITED BY DICK SCHAAP

Before the game,
Coach Lombardi took his text
from one of St. Paul's Epistles.
I don't know which one.
Maybe Vince was just using St. Paul's name
to back up his own theories,

The First Letter to Timothy opens
with thanksgiving for Paul's own conversion.
It is cited as proof that Jesus came
to save sinners, not to condemn them (1:12-17).

Next, the subject of community worship,
especially prayer and conduct in church,
is treated (2:8-15).

Third, there is an enumeration of qualities
that church leaders and helpers should have
(3:1-13).

The letter concludes
with this beautiful exhortation to Timothy:

Run your best in the race of faith,
and win eternal life for yourself. . . .

Command those
who are rich in the things of this life
not to be proud,
but to place their hope, not in such
an uncertain thing as riches, but in God. . . .
Command them . . .
to be generous and ready to share with others. . . .

Timothy,
keep safe what has been entrusted to your care.

1 TIMOTHY 6:12, 17-20

Timothy
was dedicated to the Lord's service
by the "laying on of hands"
(1 Timothy 4:14, 2 Timothy 1:6).

This ancient gesture
signified the communication of something.

In Luke 4:40, healing is communicated;
in Matthew 19:15, a blessing;
in Acts 6:6, an office;
in Acts 13:3, a commission;
in Acts 8:17, the Holy Spirit.

2 TIMOTHY

The Second Letter to Timothy
focuses on handing on the word of God.
It begins by recalling Timothy's faith,
"the kind of faith that your grandmother Lois
and your mother Eunice also had" (1:5).

The letter continues with this exhortation:

Take the teachings that you heard me
proclaim in the presence of many witnesses,
and entrust them to reliable people,
who will be able to teach others also.

2 TIMOTHY 2:2

But this will not be easy.

People will be selfish, greedy, boastful . . . ;
they will love pleasure rather than God;
they will hold to the outward form of our religion,
but reject its real power.

2 TIMOTHY 3:2-5

Then comes a warning.

The time will come
when people will not listen to sound doctrine,
but will follow their own desires
and will collect for themselves
more and more teachers who will tell them
what they are itching to hear. . . .
But you must keep control of yourself
in all circumstances; endure suffering,
do the work of a preacher of the Good News,
and perform your whole duty
as a servant of God.

2 TIMOTHY 4:3-5

Finally, the letter ends on a deeply personal note.

As for me,
the hour has come for me to be sacrificed;
the time is here for me to leave this life.
I have done my best in the race,
I have run the full distance,
and I have kept the faith.
And now there is waiting for me
the prize of victory awarded for a righteous life,
the prize which the Lord, the righteous Judge,
will give me on that Day—
and not only to me, but to all those
who wait with love for him to appear.

2 TIMOTHY 4:6-8

TITUS

Many classical Greek dramatists
avoided portraying actual violence on stage.
Rather, they suggested it
in the anguished cries of someone on stage,
watching it take place off stage.

Paul's letters are somewhat like that.
Often they reveal a person or an event
by suggestion
rather than by direct expression.
The person of Titus is a case in point.

Paul's letters
are our only source of information about Titus.
The best of these sources is 2 Corinthians.
In it Paul mentions Titus about ten times.
The overall impression conveyed
is that Titus is a close "partner" (8:23)
and a trusted envoy (7:6).

The Letter to Titus begins with this reminder:

I left you in Crete,
so that you could put in order
the things that still needed doing
and appoint church elders in every town.

TITUS 1:5

This was typical of Paul's style.
He would plow the field and sow the seed,
leaving the simpler job of cultivation to others.
Thus he told the Corinthians:

I planted the seed, Apollos watered the plant,
but it was God who made the plant grow.
The one who plants and the one who waters
really do not matter.
It is God who matters,
because he makes the plant grow.

1 CORINTHIANS 3:6-7

The Letter to Titus goes on to spell out
the qualifications for a church elder.

He must be self-controlled,
upright, holy, and disciplined.
He must hold firmly to the message. . . .
In this way he will be able . . . to show the error
of those who are opposed to it.

TITUS 1:8-9

The letter concludes:

In all things you yourself
must be an example of good behavior. . . .

Remind your people . . .
to show a gentle attitude toward everyone.
For we ourselves were once . . .
slaves to passions and pleasures of all kinds.
We spent our lives in malice and envy;
others hated us and we hated them.
But when the kindness
and love of God our Savior was revealed,
he saved us.
It was not because of any good deeds
that we ourselves had done,
but because of his own mercy
that he saved us, through the Holy Spirit,
who gives us new birth and new life
by washing us. . . .

Give at least two warnings
to the person who causes divisions,
and then have nothing more to do with him.
You know that such a person is corrupt,
and his sins prove that he is wrong. . . .

All who are with me send you greetings.
Give our greetings to our friends in the faith.

God's grace be with you all.

TITUS 2:7; 3:1-5, 10-11, 15

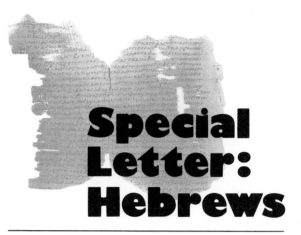

Special Letter: Hebrews

About 14,000 pieces of correspondence
from Greco-Roman times have survived the ages.
Most are penned on papyrus
and range in length from 18 to 4,134 words.

Some scholars
divide the correspondence into "letters"
(addressed to specific persons or groups)
and "epistles" (intended for the public).

The 21 pieces of correspondence
that make up a big part of the New Testament
range in length from 335 words (Philemon)
to 7,101 words (Romans).
The 13 pieces attributed to Paul (and 2-3 John)
are classified as "letters."
The remaining 6 pieces, as "epistles."

Most Bible readers
don't bother with this technical distinction.
But it may help in treating a special letter:
the Letter (Epistle) to the Hebrews.

Except for 1 John, this is the only piece
of New Testament correspondence
that does not contain

177

Who Are "the Hebrews"?

Besides the uncertainty
about the author of the Letter to the Hebrews,
there is uncertainty also
about the recipients of the letter.

Searching the Scriptures
JOHN J. DOUGHERTY

The title "to the Hebrews"
is not original but a later inference
drawn from the contents.
Pere Spicq proposes
that it was written to a community
of Jewish priests, converts from Judaism,
residing probably at Antioch.
He dates it before the destruction of the Temple,
at about A.D. 67.
The shadow of impending disaster
already loomed over Jerusalem.
It was written, he says,
to console the discouraged converts
tempted to return to their old religion.
Therefore we find emphasis
on Christ the true high priest,
and the unique sacrifice of Christ.

178

an introductory greeting and sender's name.
This has stirred up a "guessing game"
about who wrote it.
The candidates range from Paul himself
to Jude, Barnabas, Apollos,
and even Priscilla, the wife of Aquila.

Here we should recall an important fact
about New Testament authorship.

Introduction to the New Testament
RODERICK A. F. MACKENZIE

An apostle's name attached to a book
may indicate not more than
that he gave it his approval,
or simply that it is the written form
of his personal teaching.

A modern example illustrates.
The president of the United States
rarely writes his own official documents.
He merely approves what someone else
has written under his direction.
So, too, the pope and other leaders
rarely write their official documents,
but merely commission and approve them.

Concerning ancient letters, in particular,
a writer notes:

Dictionary of the Bible
JOHN L. MCKENZIE

The letter was almost always dictated to a scribe.
It appears that word for word dictation
was extremely rare;
the scribe was given instructions
and perhaps an outline.
The part of the scribe in the composition
of the New Testament epistles
was thus considerable,
since the literary formulation
was principally his work.

"The Courage to Trust"
ARDIS WHITMAN

When I was eight I went to the circus in Boston
and marveled at the trapeze artists,
soaring impossibly through space,
always catching the flying swing
from each other. "Aren't they scared?"
I whispered to my mother.

A man in the row ahead turned to answer.
"They aren't scared, honey,"
he said gently. "They trust each other."

"He used to be on the high wires himself,"
someone whispered.

The Letter to the Hebrews
is a call to trust—especially to trust Jesus.
The group to whom the letter was written
was suffering from some trial.
It was tempted to turn its back on Jesus
and give up its Christian faith.
The author exhorts the group:

Let us keep our eyes fixed on Jesus. . . .
Think of what he went through;
how he put up with so much hatred
from sinners!
So do not let yourselves become discouraged.
HEBREWS 12:2–3

This recalls Jesus' own words:

" 'No slave is greater than his master.'
If they persecuted me, they will persecute you too."
JOHN 15:20

The letter presents some concrete examples
of trust or faith in God.

It was faith
that made Abraham able to become a father,
even though he was too old. . . .

It was faith that made Abraham
offer his son Isaac in sacrifice. . . .

It was faith that made Moses . . .
suffer with God's people.

HEBREWS 11:11, 17, 24-25

The author notes
that the Christians' reason for having faith
surpasses the one Abraham and Moses had.
It is Jesus, who lives among us.

Think of Jesus,
whom God sent to be the High Priest
of the faith we profess. . . .

Our High Priest is not one
who cannot feel sympathy for our weaknesses.
On the contrary, we have a High Priest
who was tempted in every way that we are,
but did not sin.

Jesus, then,
is the High Priest that meets our needs. . . .
He is not like other high priests. . . .

The work they do as priests
is really only a copy and a shadow
of what is in heaven. . . .
Jesus has been given priestly work
which is superior to theirs,
just as the covenant which he arranged
between God and his people is a better one. . . .

The Jewish Law is not a full and faithful model
of the real things; it is only a faint outline
of the good things to come. . . .

So God does away with all the old sacrifices
and puts the sacrifice of Christ
in their place.

HEBREWS 3:1; 4:15; 7:26-27; 8:5-6; 10:1, 9

The Letter to the Hebrews
then launches into a ringing exhortation.

So let us come near to God
with a sincere heart and a sure faith. . . .
Let us hold on firmly to the hope we profess,
because we can trust God
to keep his promise. . . .
Let us not give up the habit
of meeting together, as some are doing.
Instead, let us encourage one another all the more,
since you see that the Day of the Lord
is coming nearer.

HEBREWS 10:22-25

The letter ends, echoing Genesis 18:1-8
and Matthew 25:37-40.

Remember to welcome strangers in your homes.
There were some who did that
and welcomed angels without knowing it.
Remember those who are in prison,
as though you were in prison with them.
Remember those who are suffering,
as though you were suffering as they are. . . .

For there is no permanent city for us
here on earth;
we are looking for the city which is to come. . . .

May God's grace be with you all.

HEBREWS 13:2-3, 14, 25

General Letters

Near Cripple Creek, in Colorado,
gold and tellurium
occur mixed together as telluride ore.
The refining methods of early mining camps
could not separate the two elements.
So the ore was set aside.

One day,
a miner mistook a lump of the ore for coal
and tossed it into his stove.
Later, when he took out the stove's ashes,
he found them littered with bubbles of gold.
The heat had burned away the tellurium,
leaving the gold in a purified state.
The ore that was set aside
was reworked and yielded a fortune.

The seven final letters of the New Testament
are frequently clustered together
under the title "general letters."
This is because they are intended,
for the most part, for general circulation.

Appropriately, the general letters
are put near the end of the New Testament
because five of these seven letters

(2-3 John, 2 Peter, James, and Jude)
were among the last books to be accepted
into the New Testament.

Like the telluride ore,
the true value of these books was questioned
for years.
Eventually, prayer, study, and the Holy Spirit
guided the early Christian community
to discern their inspired origin.

Unlike the Pauline letters,
which address persons or churches,
these letters address a more general audience.
A typical salutation is this one:

*Greetings to all God's people
scattered over the whole world.*

JAMES 1:1

JAMES

The play *The Teahouse of the August Moon*
opens with the spotlight focused on Sakini.
He is an interpreter for the American army
on the island of Okinawa.

Dressed in tattered clothes
and G.I. shoes, several sizes too big,
Sakini walks down to the footlights.
Hands folded, as in prayer,
he bows and introduces himself.

After describing
how Okinawa has been conquered many times
in its long history, Sakini notes
that this has helped to educate his people.
He then adds, reflectively:

*Not easy to learn.
Sometimes painful.
But pain makes man think.
Thought makes man wise.
Wisdom makes life endurable.*

This same philosophical approach to life
starts and pervades the Letter from James

Not all scholars agree
that the letter's author is James, the leader
of the Jerusalem community (Galatians 2:9).
There is considerable agreement, however,
that it was written before this James's death,
which Josephus puts around A.D. 62.

The letter
takes the form of a series of guidelines
for Christian living.
It treats such practical concerns as—

persevering under trial (1:2-18),
practicing the word (1:19-27),
avoiding social discrimination (2:1-13),
living the creed you profess (2:14-26),
controlling the tongue (3:1-12),
cultivating wisdom (3:13-18),
avoiding worldly ways (4:1-17),
giving aid to the poor (5:1-6),
practicing patience and prayer (5:7-20).

The style and tone of the document
are more in the spirit
of an oral sermon than a written letter.
Some suggest it was originally a homily
and turned into a letter by a scribe
or by a Greek-speaking disciple of James.
This would explain
the superb Greek style of the letter,
something you would not expect
from the hand of a Galilean peasant.

The sermon's tone is evident in the fact
that 54 words of the letter's 108 verses
are put in the imperative (exhortative) mood.
Similarly, the body of the letter
contains a number of sayings of Jesus
as found in Matthew's Sermon on the Mount.
Consider these:

"Happy are you
when people insult you and persecute you . . .
because you are my followers. . . .
A great reward is kept for you in heaven."

MATTHEW 5:11-12

Happy is the person
who remains faithful under trials,
because when he succeeds . . .
he will receive as his reward the life
which God has promised.

JAMES 1:12

"Happy are those who are merciful to others;
God will be merciful to them!"

MATTHEW 5:7

God will not show mercy when he judges
the person who has not been merciful.

JAMES 2:13

"Do not swear by heaven . . .
nor by earth . . . nor by Jerusalem. . . .
Just say 'Yes' or 'No'."

MATTHEW 5:34-37

Do not swear by heaven
or by earth or by anything else.
Say only "Yes" . . . and "No."

JAMES 5:12

One section of the Letter from James
deserves careful reading and reflection.
Recalling the words of Paul in Galatians 2:15-16,
it is a discussion of the relationship
between faith and works.

Some see it as opposing Paul's teaching
or, more probably,
the teaching of certain Christians
who were misinterpreting Paul.
A portion of the section reads:

What good is it for someone to say
that he has faith if his actions do not prove it?

Can that faith save him?
Suppose there are brothers or sisters
who need clothes and don't have enough to eat.
What good is there in your saying to them,
"God bless you!
Keep warm and eat well!"
if you don't give them the necessities of life?
So it is with faith:
if it is alone and includes no actions,
then it is dead.

JAMES 2:14–17

There could be no better commentary
of James's graphic passage than Paul himself.

I may have all the faith needed
to move mountains—
but if I have no love, I am nothing.

1 CORINTHIANS 13:2

Bare Facts

The *Detroit Free Press*
printed this news item under the heading
"Doesn't Believe His Own Chest":

Chicago—(AP)—*Hubert Courtney, 26,*
has something on his chest but,
the government said, pays no attention to it.
Woven into the tattooing on Courtney's torso
is the motto, "Crime does not pay."

Courtney bared
his chest before a Federal commissioner
before whom he appeared Wednesday
on a charge of interstate auto theft.

It was this kind of a contradiction
that James sought to warn Christians about
when he wrote:

Do not deceive yourselves
by just listening to his word;
instead, put it into practice.
Whoever listens to the word
but does not put it into practice
is like a man who looks in a mirror
and sees himself as he is.
He takes a good look at himself
and then goes away
and at once forgets what he looks like.

JAMES 1:22–24

I PETER

The guards amused themselves
by making the old prisoner
bark like a dog each time they approached.
Years before, the old man had been president
of a university in Holland.
Now he was behind barbed wire
in a Nazi concentration camp in Germany.

Eventually, the mistreatment and torture
took its toll on the aged prisoner.
Among his few possessions
was an old, beat-up prayer book.
The Nazis failed to notice
that the old priest had written,
between the lines of print,
the story of his suffering in prison.

> *Walking with God*
> KILIAN J. HEALY

And there, too,
he had written his last song,
a real prayer, a conversation with Jesus. . . .

"No grief shall fall my way, but I
*   Shall see Thy grief-filled eyes;*
The lonely way that Thou once walked
*   Has made me sorrow-wise. . . .*

"Stay with me, Jesus, only stay;
*   I shall not fear*
If, reaching out my hand,
*   I feel Thee near."*

The Christians
to whom Peter wrote his first letter
would have appreciated these lines.
They, also, were suffering immensely.
Peter tried to buoy their sagging spirits
by taking the same approach
that the old priest used to buoy his spirits.
Referring to the suffering, Peter writes:

God will bless you for it. . . .
Christ himself suffered for you
and left you an example,
so that you would follow in his steps.

1 PETER 2:20-21

The cause of the suffering is not specified.
But it can be inferred from what Peter says
elsewhere in the letter.

The heathen are surprised
when you do not join them
in the same wild and reckless living,
and so they insult you. . . .

Happy are you if you are insulted
because you are Christ's followers.

1 PETER 4:4, 14

Where is this discrimination taking place?
The salutation of Peter's letter
shows that one of the places is Bithynia.

This has prompted some people to suggest
that the Bithynian situation described by Peter
is the same one described by Pliny
in a letter to the Roman emperor Trajan.

Pliny, an administrator in Bithynia
around A.D.110, was plagued with problems.
His aides blamed them on a nonconformist group
called Christians.
So a number of Christians were arrested
and interrogated.
Concerning these interrogations,
Pliny wrote to Trajan:

> *Letters to Trajan*
> PLINY

I questioned them, personally,
asking them if they were Christian. . . .

Some affirmed they had once been Christians,
but no longer were. . . .

"You are the chosen race,
the King's priests, the holy nation,
God's own people, chosen to proclaim
the wonderful acts of God,
who called you out of darkness
into his own marvelous light.
At one time you were not God's people,
but now you are his people;
at one time you did not know God's mercy,
but now you have received his mercy."

1 Peter 2:9–10

They admitted meeting regularly at sunrise
on a stated day to pray to Christ as to a god. . . .
After their sunrise meeting, they broke up.
But they gathered again later on in the day
to share together in a harmless meal. . . .

I now want your personal advice.

Pliny wrote this letter around A.D. 110,
at least 40 years after the death of Peter.
This rules out the possibility that Peter
addressed the same situation as Pliny.
But it does not rule out the possibility
that Peter addressed the same situation
in an *earlier* stage of its development.

A parallel example would be
racial discrimination in the United States,
which rumbled and smoked for a full century
before erupting violently in the 1960s.

There is another fascinating possibility.

Scholars have long noted references
to baptism in Peter's first letter:
"new life" (1:3), "born again" (1:23),
and "newborn" (2:2).
These references prompt some scholars
to suggest that parts of Peter's letter
were drawn from a baptismal liturgy
that was probably used in Rome in Nero's time.

It is possible that these liturgical sections
were woven into a later letter
to encourage harrassed Christians in Bithynia.

If this is so, then the letter—
even though penned long after Peter's death—
could still claim Peter as its author,
insofar as he may have been responsible
for much of its original content.

Paul's Letters

There are some difficult things in his letters
which ignorant and unstable people
explain falsely, as they do with other passages
of the Scriptures.

2 PETER 3:16

This remarkable reference to Paul's letters
in the Second Letter from Peter
is extremely valuable for two reasons.

First, it presumes a body of Paul's letters
that is well known and frequently referred to.

Second,
it implies that Paul's letters were esteemed
as having the status of Scripture itself.

Some scholars think that these two facts,
along with others in Peter's second letter,
demand that we date it after Peter's lifetime.
In other words,
such a sophisticated acceptance of Paul's letters
would have taken years to develop.
Thus, the letter may have been written by
a later hand and attributed to Peter.
Defending this possibility, an author writes:

Dictionary of the Bible
JOHN L. MCKENZIE

The attribution to Peter may indicate
that the author had been a disciple of Peter
who attempted to answer the question
of the delay of the Parousia [Second Coming]
in terms which he remembered as those of Peter.

Such an attribution would not have been
frowned upon in the ancient world.

2 PETER

Time tends to color events.
Whether it be John Kennedy's assassination
or the Vietnam War,
time invariably tends to generate
its own slants and new theories.

Something like this
began to happen in early Christian times.
Some people began changing or slanting
things that Jesus said or did.
Commenting on these people, Peter writes:

They have left the straight path
and have lost their way. . . .

It would have been much better for them
never to have known the way of righteousness
than to know it and then turn away
from the sacred command that was given them.

2 PETER 2:15, 21

One area upon which some Christians
were casting doubts was Jesus' Second Coming.
They expected Jesus to come quickly.
But when Jesus was slow in coming,
they became even slower in believing
that Jesus would ever come.
Addressing himself to Jesus' "slowness,"
Peter writes:

My dear friends!
There is no difference in the Lord's sight
between one day and a thousand years;
to him the two are the same.
The Lord is not slow
to do what he has promised, as some think.
Instead, he is patient with you,
because he does not want anyone
to be destroyed,
but wants all to turn away from their sins.

2 PETER 3:8-9

Reassuring those who may have been shaken
by the doubters or their false teaching,
Peter writes:

We have not depended on made-up stories
in making known to you
the mighty coming of our Lord Jesus Christ.
With our own eyes we saw his greatness.
We were there when he was given honor
and glory by God the Father,
when the voice came to him
from the Supreme Glory, saying,
"This is my own dear Son,
with whom I am pleased!"
We ourselves
heard this voice coming from heaven,
when we were with him on the holy mountain.

2 PETER 1:16–18

Peter concludes his brief letter:

And so, my friends, as you wait for that Day,
do your best to be pure and faultless
in God's sight and to be at peace with him.
Look on our Lord's patience
as the opportunity he is giving you to be saved. . . .

To him be the glory, now and forever!
Amen.

2 PETER 3:14–18

I JOHN

Jesus called John and his brother James
the "sons of thunder" (Mark 3:17).
The nickname may have been sparked
by the brothers' explosive response
to Samaritans
who barred Jesus from their town (Luke 9:54).

John (with Peter and James)
was with Jesus on several key occasions
(Luke 8:51; 9:28; Mark 14:33).

Many believe it was this same John
who wrote the last three "general letters."
Others, for involved reasons, suggest
it was a disciple of John's using his name.

The First Letter of John
lacks several conventional letter marks.
For example,
there is no sender's or receiver's name,
no introductory salutation,
and no final greetings to individuals.

But this lack is more than made up for
by the letter's inspirational beginning.

We write to you about the Word of life,
which has existed from the very beginning.
We have heard it,
and we have seen it with our eyes;
yes, we have seen it, and our hands have touched it.
When this life became visible, we saw it;
so we speak of it and tell you about
the eternal life which was with the Father
and was made known to us.
What we have seen and heard
we announce to you also,
so that you will join with us
in the fellowship that we have with the Father
and with his Son Jesus Christ.
We write this
in order that our joy may be complete.

1 JOHN 1:1–4

The literary kinship
between the prologue of John's first letter
and the prologue of John's Gospel is striking.
So is the theological kinship
between the letter's stress on witness
and the Gospel's stress—
woman's witness (John 4:39), Father's (5:37),
Scripture's (5:39), Spirit's (15:26),
evangelist's (21:24), to cite a few.

The content of the letter
indicates that false teachers had infiltrated
some Christian communities.

I am writing this to you
about those who are trying to deceive you.

1 JOHN 2:26

John identifies these teachers, collectively,
as the "Enemy of Christ"—or, as some Bibles
translate it, "Antichrist" (1 John 2:18, 22; 4:3).
This expression means
"one who opposes Christ [the Messiah]" or

"one who replaces Christ" (Matthew 24:24,
2 Thessalonians 2:3-8).

What were these false teachers saying?

For one thing, they denied that
Jesus is Messiah (1 John 2:22), Son (2:23),
and a "human being" (4:2).

They claimed access to a special spirit
and a special knowledge from God (4:1-6).
Scholars generally agree the teachers
had adopted some form of Gnosticism
("knowledge"), an early church heresy.

"My children,
our love should not be just words and talk;
it must be true love,
which shows itself in action."
1 John 3:18

Although the various twists Gnosticism took
make it hard to define, this may be said.
Gnostics believed the created world was evil.
They saw it as separated from and opposed to
the world of the spirit.
God lived in the world of the spirit
and had no dealings with the world of matter,
which was created by an inferior being.

Salvation for the Gnostics
consisted in "knowledge" of the two worlds
and of how to escape from the material world
to the spiritual world at death.

Directing his attack
at the claims of these teachers, John writes:

Do not believe all who claim to have the Spirit,
but test them to find out
if the spirit they have comes from God. . . .
Anyone who acknowledges
that Jesus Christ came as a human being
has the Spirit. . . .
God has given us eternal life,
and this life has its source in his Son. . . .
Whoever does not have the Son of God
does not have life.

1 JOHN 4:1-2; 5:11-12

The First Letter of John
is of special value to us for two reasons.
First, it is a powerful affirmation
of the humanity and divinity of Jesus.
Second, it is a strong affirmation
of the close link between Christian morality
and Christian doctrine. We read:

Now the message
that we have heard from his Son
and announce is this: God is light,
and there is no darkness at all in him. . . .

Whoever loves his brother
lives in the light. . . .

But whoever hates his brother
is in the darkness. . . .

Dear friends, let us love one another,
because love comes from God. . . .

God is love, and whoever lives in love
lives in union with God
and God lives in union with him. . . .

If someone says he loves God,
but hates his brother, he is a liar.
For he cannot love God, whom he has not seen,
if he does not love his brother,
whom he has seen.
The command that Christ has given us
is this: whoever loves God
must love his brother also. . . .

My children,
keep yourselves safe from false gods!

1 JOHN 1:5; 2:10-11; 4:7, 16, 20-21; 5:21

2-3 JOHN

John's final two letters
have the conventional marks of a letter.
Both come from the hand of "the Elder"
and are addressed to churches.

The first of these letters is addressed to
"the dear Lady and to her children,"
probably a church in Asia Minor.
The second is addressed to Gaius,
but it is intended for a church
whose leader had broken off with John.

Both letters are little more than notes.
The first appeals to church members
to continue in their love for one another
and to be alert for false teachers.
The second praises Gaius
for his service and warns him of Diotrephes,
the errant church leader.

189

JUDE

Once Jesus told a parable
about a farmer who planted a field.
At night an enemy slipped into the field
and oversowed it with weeds.
Later on, when the servants saw
the weeds growing alongside the grain,
they asked the farmer
if they should uproot them.

" 'No,' he answered,
'because as you gather the weeds
you might pull up some of the wheat
along with them.
Let the wheat and the weeds
both grow together until harvest.
Then I will tell the harvest workers
to pull up the weeds first,
tie them in bundles and burn them.' "

MATTHEW 13:29-30

The Letter from Jude concerns a situation
like the one described in Jesus' parable.
The author writes:

Some godless people
have slipped in unnoticed among us,
persons who distort the message
about the grace of our God
in order to excuse their immoral ways.

JUDE 4

Jude makes a perceptive observation
when he says the "godless people" distort
the truth "to excuse their immoral ways."

When one's belief and behavior clash,
one can become a Dr. Jekyll and Mr. Hyde.
One can split down the middle,
believing one way and behaving another.

Since living in this way is uncomfortable,
people try to resolve the conflict.

First they try to change their behavior
to conform to their belief.
If they can't do this,
they change their belief to fit their behavior.

The "godless people" picked the latter path.
Their rejection of Jesus
seems to have been more at a practical level
than at a theoretical one.

Jude uses several vivid metaphors
to warn about the spiritual deadness
and the tragic destiny of these people.

They are like clouds carried along by the wind,
but bringing no rain.
They are like trees that bear no fruit. . . .
They are like wandering stars,
for whom God has reserved a place forever
in the deepest darkness.

JUDE 12-13

Jude ends his letter, telling his readers:

Pray in the power of the Holy Spirit,
and keep yourselves in the love of God,
as you wait for our Lord Jesus Christ
in his mercy to give you eternal life.

JUDE 20-21

Jude identifies himself only as a "servant
of Jesus Christ, and brother of James."
Since he does not say
he was one of "the twelve," scholars assume
he was not Jude the apostle (Luke 6:16),
but another Jude (Mark 6:3),
who wrote between A.D. 60 and A.D. 90.

"They are like trees
that bear no fruit . . .
trees that have been pulled up by the roots
and are completely dead."
Jude 12

Special Book: Revelation

"Study the book of Revelation.
Study it as you have never studied it before.
Then go out to your churches and preach it.
It is the one book above all others
that demands our study today."
The speaker was Wilbur Smith,
eminent Presbyterian scholar and minister. . . .

He continued, with intense earnestness,
"I have never . . . felt so strongly
about anything as I now feel about this.
Please! Please! Study this book."

Orley M. Berg

The Book of Revelation is addressed
to Christians being persecuted for their faith.
It attributes a series of visions to "John,"
a persecuted Christian
living in exile on a Mediterranean island.

John refers to himself four times by name
but gives us no personal information.
Tradition identifies him as John the apostle,
but there is no certitude about this.

Nor is there certitude about the book's date.
Some place it
during Nero's persecution around A.D. 64;
others, during Domitian's around A.D. 90.

As for John's visions,
there is, likewise, no certitude as to whether
they are real experiences or literary devices
to convey John's revelation from God.

John describes his visions in a complex way,
weaving together three ancient literary styles:
apocalyptic, prophetic, and epistolary.

The apocalyptic ("veiled") style appears,
especially, in the book's wide use of symbolism.
It ranges from bodily features like eyes,
standing for knowledge (5:6),
to colors like white, meaning victory (4:4),
to numbers like seven, symbolizing fullness
(used 54 times in the book).

The prophetic style is evident in the fact
that John, like the prophets of old,
is called in an "inaugural vision" (1:9-20)
and ordered to communicate what he "hears"
(like the prophets of old) 11 different times.
Furthermore, John speaks of "prophecy"
in several places (for example, 1:3; 19:10; 22:7).

Finally, the book's epistolary style
shows up not only in the seven messages
to the seven churches (2:1-3:22)
but also in the letterlike salutation
and conclusion of the book (1:4-6; 22:21).

SEVEN LETTERS

John begins:

This book is the record of the events
that Jesus Christ revealed.
God gave him this revelation
in order to show to his servants
what must happen very soon.

"A few yards away
rose the stately steps of a temple
leading upward to—nothing."
H. V. Morton

So Lonely, So Silent . . .

The modern tourist
strolling among the ruins of Ephesus today
should put down his camera long enough
to read from the Book of Revelation:

To the angel of the church in Ephesus write:

*"This is the message
from the one who holds the seven stars
in his right hand and who walks among
the seven gold lampstands. . . .
If you don't turn from your sins,
I will come to you
and take your lampstand from its place."*

REVELATION 2:1, 5

Apparently the letter went unheeded.
Today Ephesus is a pile of ruins.
A modern journalist describes his visit
to the ancient site.

In the Steps of St. Paul
H. V. MORTON

*Sitting on a fallen pillar,
I ate the sandwiches I had brought with me.
A few yards away rose the stately steps
of a temple leading upward to—nothing.
Little yellow flowers grew out of cracks
in the marble.
A fragment of stone,
bearing the name of Augustus Caesar,
lay upside down,
and it was scored with hundreds
of deep scratches, as if someone
had been sharpening a knife on it. . . .
So lonely, so silent is Ephesus.*

*Christ made these things known
to his servant John by sending his angel
to him,
and John has told all that he has seen.
This is his report
concerning the message from God
and the truth revealed by Jesus Christ. . . .*

*I heard a loud voice,
that sounded like a trumpet, speaking behind me.
It said,
"Write down what you see, and send the book
to the churches in these seven cities:
Ephesus, Smyrna, Pergamum, Thyatira,
Sardis, Philadelphia, and Laodicea."*

REVELATION 1:1–2, 10–11

193

"'To the angel of the church in Sardis write:
... Wake up, and strengthen
what you still have before it dies completely.'"
Revelation 3:1–2

The ruins on the valley floor
are all that remains of ancient Sardis today.

John turned around.
He saw a figure standing amid seven gold
lampstands, symbolizing the seven churches.
The face of the figure
"was as bright as the midday sun,"
and in his right hand were seven stars,
symbolizing the angels of the seven churches.
The figure said:

*"Don't be afraid. . . . I was dead,
but now I am alive forever and ever."*
REVELATION 1:17–18

The figure then dictated seven letters,
one for each of the seven churches.
The message of each letter was the same.
It rebuked the church for past failures
and exhorted the church to future fidelity.

SEVEN SEALS

John continues:

*At this point I had another vision
and saw an open door in heaven.*
REVELATION 4:1

On a throne sat a figure with shining face.
He was encircled by 24 elders
dressed in white and wearing gold crowns.

"Surrounding the throne on each of its sides,
were four living creatures" (4:6).
One looked like a lion,
the second like a bull,
the third had the face of a man,
the fourth resembled an eagle in flight.
The creatures sang:

194

"Holy, holy, holy, is the Lord God Almighty, who was, who is, and who is to come."

REVELATION 4:8

John's description of this second vision respects the Jewish custom of not specifying God. The throne and the posture of the figure suggest his dual role: king and judge (Matthew 25:31-46).

The 24 elders suggest the leaders of Israel's 12 tribes and their successors, the 12 apostles (Matthew 19:28). All of God's chosen people are represented.

The four creatures recall Ezekiel 1:10. They suggest the fullness of God's creation, just as the elders suggest the fullness of God's people.

Since the second century, Christian tradition has used the four creatures (Revelation 4:7) to symbolize the four evangelists.

The desert lion symbolizes Mark, whose Gospel opens with a "voice in the desert."

The sacrificial ox symbolizes Luke, whose Gospel opens with sacrifice in the temple.

The man symbolizes Matthew, who opens with a record of Jesus' human ancestry.

The eagle symbolizes John, who opens with a hymn to Jesus, who alone looks on God's face, just as the eagle alone (according to folklore) looks on the sun's face.

The panel shown here is from the main doorway of the Cathedral of Chartres in France.

The four creatures represent
what is most splendid in animate life:
the lion—nobility; the bull—strength;
the man—wisdom; the eagle—swiftness.
The whole of creation is thus represented
before the throne of God.

The last line of the creature's song,
"who was, who is, and who is to come,"
recalls the "I-am-who-am" title
applied to God in Exodus 3:14.
It suggests the mystery of God's eternity
as closely as human conceptualization can.

Next, John saw a Lamb
that seemed "to have been killed" (5:6).
The Lamb had seven horns and seven eyes.
It was given a scroll
by the figure seated on the center throne.
Then singing broke out. John says:

I heard . . . all living beings in the universe—
and they were singing:

"To him who sits on the throne and to the Lamb,
be praise and honor, and glory and might,
forever and ever!"

The four living creatures answered, "Amen!"
And the elders fell down and worshiped.
REVELATION 5:13–14

Reference to the "Lamb"
(the first of 28 such references in the book)
recalls the words spoken of Jesus
by John the Baptist at the Jordan River:
"There is the Lamb of God,
who takes away the sin of the world" (John 1:29).

The title recalls, also, the words
spoken of the Suffering Servant of Yahweh
by the prophet Isaiah:

"Like a lamb about to be slaughtered . . .
he never said a word" (Isaiah 53:7).

The seven horns and the seven eyes
suggest the fullness (seven = fullness)
of power (horns) and knowledge (eyes)
that belong to the victorious Lamb of God.

The taking of the scroll
implies the accession of the Lamb to the throne.
The risen Jesus
shares his Father's kingship and power forever.
The event recalls the last line
of the last letter dictated in the first vision:
"I have been victorious and now I sit
by my Father on his throne" (3:21).

The scroll that the Lamb was given
was bound tightly by seven seals.
John watched
as the Lamb began to break the seals.

The breaking of each of the first four seals
caused a horse and a rider to appear.

The first horse was white,
and its rider carried a bow in his hand.
The second horse was red,
and its rider carried a sword in his hand.
The third horse was black,
and its rider carried a pair of scales.
The fourth horse was pale-colored,
and its rider bore the name "Death."

They were given authority
over one fourth of the earth, to kill
by means of war, famine, disease,
and wild animals.
REVELATION 6:8

The instruments of the "four horsemen"
are symbolic.
The bow suggests the Parthians
(their main weapon), Rome's chief rival.

The sword suggests war.
The scales (weighing food) suggests famine.

The evils appear sequenced:
war brings famine, famine brings disease,
disease brings death and scavenger animals.
The colors seem coded:
white (victor), red (war), black (death),
pale-colored (rotting flesh).

When the fifth seal was broken,
it revealed a great throng of people
who had been persecuted for their faith.
They asked judgment on their persecutors
but were told to be patient a while longer
till the quota of martyrs was completed.

Then the sixth seal was broken.
Immediately the earth quaked,
the sun blackened, the moon reddened,
and the stars fell from the sky.
The powerful ones on earth
shouted to the mountains:

"Fall on us and hide us
from the eyes of the one who sits on the throne
and from the anger of the Lamb!"

REVELATION 6:16

Then four angels appeared.
They were empowered to devastate the earth.
But before they could do anything,
a fifth angel appeared and said:

"Do not harm the earth . . .
until we mark the servants of our God
with a seal on their foreheads."

REVELATION 7:3

The number sealed was 144,000.
This number
conveys symbolic, not numerical, value.
It has been variously interpreted.
One possible interpretation is the following:

Twelve (the sacred number)
squared and multiplied by one thousand
represents the totality
of all who have been faithful to Christ
(the new Israel).

The protective mark recalls
that ancients protected their property
by marking or sealing it with their rings.

Paul uses this same "sealing" imagery
in 2 Corinthians 1:22 and Ephesians 4:30.

Then John saw an enormous crowd of people
standing before the Lamb's throne.
They were the survivors of the persecution.
An elder told John:

"Never again will they hunger or thirst;
neither sun nor any scorching heat
will burn them. . . .
And God will wipe away every tear
from their eyes."

When the Lamb broke open the seventh seal,
there was silence in heaven for about half an hour.

REVELATION 7:16-8:1

This last sentence brings to an abrupt end
the vision of the seven seals.
The vision's overall meaning is contained
in the single word *silence.*

Silence was a code word
for a number of the Old Testament prophets.
Consider Zechariah 2:13:

Be silent, everyone, in the presence of the LORD,
for he is coming from his holy dwelling place.

And Zephaniah 1:7:

The day when the LORD will sit in judgment is near;
so be silent in his presence.

SEVEN TRUMPETS

Then John saw another vision.
Seven angels began blowing seven trumpets
in successive order (8:2-11:19).

The first trumpet blast touched off a fire
that destroyed a third of the earth.
The second blast turned a third of the sea to blood.
The third blast
contaminated a third of the earth's waters.
The fourth blast caused the heavenly bodies
to lose a third of their brightness.
The fifth blast unleashed a plague of locusts.
The sixth blast caused fire, smoke, and
sulphur to kill a third of the earth's people.

But those who survived these cosmic calamities
did not repent their evil ways.

Lastly, John was told to measure the temple
to prepare for the coming of "two witnesses,"
who will proclaim God's message for 1,260 days.

After this a beast will slay them.
But after three and a half days,
God will raise them up to heaven.
The vision then ends abruptly.

The seventh angel blew his trumpet,
and there were loud voices in heaven, saying,
"The power to rule over the world
belongs now to our Lord and his Messiah."
REVELATION 11:15

The message of the seven trumpets
echoes the message of the seven seals.
The seven calamities recall the Egyptian plagues
(Exodus 7-10), preludes to God's deliverance
of his people in Old Testament times.

The "two witnesses"
have been variously interpreted.
Some scholars identify them as Peter and Paul,
builders of the "new temple," Christ's church.

DRAGON AND BEASTS

Next, John looked to the sky.
There he saw a woman
"whose dress was the sun
and who had the moon under her feet
and a crown of twelve stars
on her head" (12:1).
She was giving birth.

A dragon with seven heads
and a crown on each head
tried to destroy the newborn baby.
But the child was snatched to safety,
and the woman escaped into a desert.

Then a great battle took place
between the dragon "with his angels"
and "Michael and his angels" (12:7).

The dragon's forces
were defeated and cast down to earth.
They pursued the woman, unsuccessfully,
into the desert.

The identity of the woman is debated.
Some see her as Mary;
others, as Israel—
both mothers of the Messiah,
in a true sense.

Like the infant Moses (Exodus 2:1-10)
and the infant Jesus (Matthew 2:13-15),
the infant church will be rescued
from those who seek to destroy her.

Reference to "Michael and his angels"
recalls the Book of Daniel.
Speaking of the worst catastrophe
"since nations first came into existence,"
the book says:
" 'At that time the great angel Michael,
who guards your people, will appear' "
(Daniel 12:1).

When the dragon failed
in its pursuit of the woman into the desert
(as Pharaoh failed against Israel,
Exodus 14:28),
the dragon pursued the woman's descendants,
the church—those "faithful to the truth
revealed by Jesus" (12:17).

This vision is followed by another one
of a beast rising up out of the sea.
Again, the dragon plays a role in the vision.
It empowered the beast
to war against God's people
and to defeat them for 42 months.

Then a second beast rose from the earth.
It breathed life back into the first beast.
And it killed all who refused to worship it.
The beast had a number, 666,
which stood for its name (13:18).

The beast image
(intended to be a Roman emperor)
derives from the Book of Daniel (7:17-26).

The time image (period of distress)
derives from Daniel, also (7:25),
and repeats Revelation 11:3, 12:6, and 12:14.

The 666 image (Roman emperor's name)
is frequently identified with Nero Caesar
(*nwrwn qsr*, in Hebrew).
The letter values total 666
(50 + 200 + 6 + 50 + 100 + 60 + 200).

Nero was the first emperor to persecute
the Christians.
He came back to life again in Domitian,
the second emperor to persecute them.

Then John saw angels in the sky.
One was saying in a loud voice:
"The time has come;
the earth is ripe for the harvest" (14:15)

SEVEN BOWLS

John's next vision
centers around seven angels in heaven
who were given seven golden bowls.
John says:

*Then I heard a loud voice
speaking from the temple to the seven angels:
"Go and pour out the seven bowls
of God's anger on the earth!"*

REVELATION 16:1

The first bowl produced sores on those
who bore the mark of the beast.
The second bowl contaminated earth's seas
so that all living things in them died.
The third bowl contaminated earth's rivers
and springs, turning them into blood.
"They poured out the blood of God's people . . .
you have given them blood to drink" (16:6).

The fourth bowl burned the people,
but they would not turn from their sins.
The fifth bowl cast the beast's kingdom
into utter darkness.
The sixth bowl caused the "kings of the world"
to mass for battle at Armageddon.
The seventh bowl triggered an earthquake
that devoured islands and mountains
and caused huge hailstones to bombard
the earth.

Like the visions
of the seven seals and the seven trumpets,
the vision of the seven bowls
unfolds with a series of cosmic calamities.
Unlike the earlier two visions, however,
it does not advance beyond this point.
The remaining pattern is so familiar
that there is no need to retrace it a third time.

In any event, one thing is crystal clear:
It is time for God to act.

How to Interpret Revelation?

Some tourists
were exploring New Mexico's Carlsbad Caverns.
While they were in the depths of the caves,
the lights went off.

Among those trapped in frightening darkness
were two children.
Suddenly, the young child began to cry.
The older one was heard to say tenderly:
"Don't cry! There is a man up there
who knows how to turn the lights on again."

Everyone agrees
that one message of the Book of Revelation
is akin to the older child's reassurance
to the younger child.

The Book of Revelation assures Christians
that the suffering happening to them now
happened to Jesus also.
If they stand fast in the storm as Jesus did,
they will be victorious as Jesus was.
But is this the *only* message of the book?

"There is a man up there
who knows how to turn the lights on again."

This raises the question
of how the book should be interpreted.

Four basic approaches
to interpreting the Book of Revelation
have emerged over the centuries.

The first may be called the *past* approach.
It holds that all the visions of the book
concern the persecution of Christians
by Romans in the first century.
They protest the situation
and predict God's imminent intervention.

The second, the *panorama-of-history* approach,
holds that the visions of the book
set forth a grandiose sweep of all history
starting with the first-century persecutions
and ending with the culmination of history.

The third, the *end-of-the-world* approach,
holds that the visions after chapter four
describe events
that will signal and accompany the end times.

The fourth, the *exhortational* approach,
holds that the book is a poetic creation
exhorting first-century Christians to hold fast
to their faith in their hour of trial.

The value of each approach is clear.

The first makes the book
a guide to Christians of its own age.
The second makes it a guide to every age.
The third makes it a guide
to those who will be living in the last age.
The fourth makes the book a guide
to Christians of all ages.
They are to trust God and live as Christians,
regardless of what trials they may encounter.

No view is completely satisfactory.
Perhaps the correct view
combines features from all four views.

THE END

John says:

*After this I saw
another angel coming down out of heaven. . . .
He cried out in a loud voice:
"She has fallen!
Great Babylon [Rome] has fallen!"*
REVELATION 18:1-2

Then heaven opened
and revealed a rider on a white horse.
He bore the name
"King of kings and Lord of lords."
John says:

*Then I saw the beast
and the kings of the earth and their armies
gathered to fight
against the one who was riding the horse.*
REVELATION 19:19

But the battle ended quickly.
The beast and the kings and their armies
were no match for the rider on the white horse.

Next, an angel came down from heaven,
seized the dragon,
and confined him for a "thousand years."
Then the just souls rose from the dead
and ruled with Christ for a "thousand years."
John comments:

*This is the first raising of the dead. . . .
The second death has no power over them.*
REVELATION 20:5-6

When the thousand-year period ended,
Satan went about on earth again
and assembled a vast army of nations,
"that is, Gog and Magog" (20:8)
to war against God's people.

201

But fire came down from heaven
and destroyed them. Then the Devil ...
was thrown into the lake of fire ...
forever and ever.

REVELATION 20:9-10

John concludes:

Then I saw a great white throne
and the one who sits on it.
Earth and heaven fled from his presence
and were seen no more.
And I saw the dead, great and small alike,
standing before the throne. . . .
And all were judged
according to what they had done.
Then death and the world of the dead
were thrown into the lake of fire.
(This lake of fire is the second death.)
Whoever did not have his name written
in the book of the living
was thrown into the lake of fire.

REVELATION 20:11-15

The "first raising of the dead" is debated.

Inspired by Ezekiel 37:1-14 and Isaiah 26:19,
some interpret it
to symbolize the recovery of the church
after the Roman persecution.

The "thousand years," then, symbolizes
the reign of Jesus' church on earth
from the fall of Rome to the final judgment
(20:11-15).

The "first death" is the loss of earthly life;
the "second death" is the loss of eternal life.

"Gog and Magog" echo Ezekiel 38-39,
where a mysterious leader of the future,
Gog of Magog (unidentified region on earth),
will subject God's people to a final ordeal.
Here they symbolize the godless nations
arrayed against the church in the end times.

THE BEGINNING

The old world has vanished.
The enemies of God have departed. John writes:

Then I saw a new heaven and a new earth.
The first heaven and the first earth
disappeared, and the sea vanished.
And I saw the Holy City, the new Jerusalem,
coming down out of heaven from God,
prepared and ready,
like a bride dressed to meet her husband.
I heard a loud voice speaking from the throne:
"Now God's home is with mankind!
He will live with them . . . and he will be their God.
He will wipe away all tears from their eyes.
There will be no more death, no more grief
or crying or pain.
The old things have disappeared." . . .

The city's wall
was built on twelve foundation stones,
on which were written the names
of the twelve apostles of the Lamb. . . .

I did not see a temple in the city, because its temple
is the Lord God Almighty and the Lamb.
The city has no need
of the sun or the moon to shine on it,
because the glory of God shines on it,
and the Lamb is its lamp.

REVELATION 21:1-4, 14, 22-23

Then John hears the voice of Jesus:

"Listen!" says Jesus, "I am coming soon!
I will bring my rewards with me,
to give to each one according to what he has done.
I am the first and the last,
the beginning and the end."

REVELATION 22:12-13

John answers:
Come, Lord Jesus!

REVELATION 22:20

Come, Lord Jesus!

REFERENCE NOTES

Part One

R. D. Linder and R. V. Pierard, "The Cross Over East Germany," *Christianity Today*, October 25, 1974, p. 46.

C. K. Barrett, *Luke the Historian in Recent Study* (Philadelphia: Fortress Press, 1970), p. 57.

Robert J. Karras, *What Are They Saying about Luke and Acts?* (New York: Paulist Press, 1979), p. 113.

Irene Champernowne, *The One and Only Me* (Allen, Tex.: Argus Communications, 1975), p. 58.

Robert J. Karras, *What Are They Saying about Luke and Acts?* pp. 115-16.

Neal M. Flanagan, *The Acts of the Apostles*, New Testament Reading Guide Series (Collegeville, Minn.: Liturgical Press, 1960), p. 13.

Richard J. Dillon and Joseph A. Fitzmyer, "Acts of the Apostles," in *The Jerome Biblical Commentary*, ed. Raymond E. Brown et al. (Englewood Cliffs, N.J.: Prentice-Hall, 1968), p. 166.

John L. McKenzie, *Dictionary of the Bible* (New York: Macmillan, 1965), p. 11.

Peter Matthiessen, *The Snow Leopard* (New York: Viking Press, 1978), p. 22.

George A. Buttrick, ed., *The Interpreter's Bible*, Vol. IX, *The Acts, Romans* (Nashville: Abingdon Press, 1954), p. 58.

Edgar Guest, "Sermons We See," in *Collected Verse of Edgar A. Guest* (Chicago: Reilly & Lee, 1934), p. 599.

Robert Frost, "A Masque of Reason," in *The Poetry of Robert Frost*, ed. Edward Connery Lathem (New York: Holt, Rinehart and Winston, 1969), p. 481.

George A. Buttrick, ed., *The Interpreter's Bible*, p. 62.

John L. McKenzie, *Dictionary of the Bible*, p. 153.

Robert Rybicki, personal communication.

F. B. Rhein, *An Analytical Approach to the New Testament* (Woodbury, N.Y.: Barron's Educational Series, 1966), p. 144.

Michael Hirsley, "Christian Commune in Evanston," *Chicago Tribune*, March 5, 1978.

Communist Youth, *Presbyterian Survey*, February 1961, p. 1.

Neal M. Flanagan, *The Acts of the Apostles*, p. 21.

Carlos Mesters, "The Bible, the People's Book," *Maryknoll* Magazine, June 1981, pp. 48-50.

William Barclay, *The Acts of the Apostles*, rev. ed. (Philadelphia: Westminster Press, 1976), p. 50.

H. G. Wells, "The Three Greatest Men in History," *Reader's Digest*, May 1935.

Neal M. Flanagan, *The Acts of the Apostles*, p. 27.

Part Two

Douglas Hyde, *I Believed* (London: William Heinemann, 1950), p. 249.

Peter Bamm, *Early Sites of Christianity*, trans. Stanley Godman (New York: Pantheon Books, 1957), p. 180.

Edgar J. Goodspeed, *Paul* (Nashville: Abingdon Press, 1947), p. 21.

Carlo Carretto, *Letters from the Desert*, trans. Rose Mary Hancock (New York: Pillar Books, 1976), pp. 12-14.

Bruce Catton, *This Hallowed Ground: The Story of the Union Side of the Civil War* (New York: Doubleday & Co., 1956), pp. 160-61.

William Barclay, *The Acts of the Apostles*, p. 79.

Frank Hoare, *Walking Among Strangers* (St. Columbans, Nebr.: Columban Fathers, n.d.).

F. J. Foakes-Jackson, *The Acts of the Apostles* (New York: Harper and Brothers, 1931), p. 100.

William Barclay, *The Master's Men* (Nashville: Abingdon Press, 1969), p. 103.

Part Three

William M. Ramsay, *St. Paul the Traveller and the Roman Citizen* (Grand Rapids: Baker Book House, 1962; reprinted from the printing made in 1897 by Hodder and Stoughton, London), p. 74.

John Stott, "Following Paul in Turkey," *Christian Century*, July 21, 1978, p. 36.

H. V. Morton, *In the Steps of St. Paul* (New York: Dodd, Mead & Co., 1936), p. 216.

William Barclay, *Ambassador for Christ* (Valley Forge, Pa.: Judson Press, 1974), pp. 86-87.

Benjamin Willard Robinson, *The Life of Paul*, 2d ed. (Chicago: University of Chicago Press, 1928), p. 89.

Part Four

Charles N. Barnard, "Back to Bataan," *Reader's Digest*, December 1980, pp. 58-69 (condensed from *Prime Time*, August 1980).

William Barclay, *The Acts of the Apostles*, p. 122.

Malcolm Muggeridge and Alec Vidler, *Paul: Envoy Extraordinary* (New York: Harper & Row, 1972), pp. 95-96.

William Barclay, *The Acts of the Apostles*, p. 124.

F. F. Bruce, *Paul: Apostle of the Heart Set Free* (Grand Rapids: Wm. B. Eerdmans, 1977), p. 226.

Stewart Perowne, *The Journeys of St. Paul* (Feltham, Middlesex, England: Hamlyn Publishing Group Limited, 1973), p. 8.

H. V. Morton, *In the Steps of St. Paul*, pp. 290-92.

Calvin J. Roetzel, *The Letters of Paul* (Atlanta: John Knox Press, 1975), p. 10.

Giuseppe Ricciotti, *Paul the Apostle*, trans. Alba I. Zizzamia (Milwaukee: Bruce Publishing Co., 1953), p. 326.

Benjamin Willard Robinson, *The Life of Paul*, p. 224.

Part Five

Morton Kelsey, *Dreams: A Way to Listen to God* (New York: Paulist Press, 1978), pp. 29-30.

George Milligan, ed. and trans., *Selections from the Greek Papyri*, No. 47 (Freeport, N.Y.: Books for Libraries Press, 1910), pp. 113-14.

Malcolm Muggeridge and Alec Vidler, *Paul: Envoy Extraordinary*, p. 29.

James Stewart, "This Was My Father," as told to Floyd Miller, *McCalls Magazine*, May 1964, p. 210.

H. V. Morton, *In the Steps of St. Paul*, p. 394.

Max Pauli, "Prayer on a Pencil," in *Prayers for the Time Being* (Liguori, Mo.: Liguori Publications, 1971), p. 155.

Benjamin Willard Robinson, *The Life of Paul*, p. 173.

James B. Irwin with William A. Emerson, Jr., *To Rule the Night: The Discovery Voyage of Astronaut Jim Irwin* (Philadelphia: A. J.

Holman, div. of J. B. Lippincott, 1973), pp. 17-18, 22.

Robert M. Herhold, *Moments of Grace* (Philadelphia: Fortress Press, 1981), p. 16.

Part Six

Benjamin Willard Robinson, *The Life of Paul*, p. 194.

Dietrich Bonhoeffer, "Night Voices," trans. Keith R. Crim in *I Loved This People* (Atlanta: John Knox Press, 1965), pp. 51-58.

George Seaver, *The Faith of Edward Wilson* (London: John Murray, 1948), p. 44.

William M. Ramsay, *St. Paul the Traveller and the Roman Citizen*, p. 314.

William Barclay, *Ambassador for Christ*, pp. 144-45.

William M. Ramsay, *St. Paul the Traveller and the Roman Citizen*, pp. 37, 38.

Stewart Perowne, *The Journeys of St. Paul*, pp. 121-22.

Letters of Fyodor Michailovitch Dostoevsky to His Family and Friends, trans. Ethel Colburn Mayne (London: Chatto & Windus, 1914), pp. 60-61.

Ralph L. Woods, reported in *The Guideposts Treasury of Faith* (New York: Doubleday & Co., 1970), p. 161.

John J. Dougherty, *Searching the Scriptures* (New York: Doubleday & Co., 1959), pp. 204-5.

"30 Years Later, a Japanese Surrenders," *Chicago Sun-Times*, March 11, 1974.

G. Ernest Wright, *Biblical Archaeology*, rev. and exp. ed. (Philadelphia: Westminster Press, 1962), p. 249.

John L. McKenzie, *Dictionary of the Bible*, p. 240.

Alan Artner, "Art Institute's New 'Jewels,'" *Chicago Tribune*, May 1, 1981.

John L. McKenzie, *Dictionary of the Bible*, p. 645.

Jerry Kramer, *Instant Replay: The Green Bay Diary of Jerry Kramer*, ed. Dick Schaap (New York: World Publishing Co., 1968), p. 233.

John J. Dougherty, *Searching the Scriptures*, p. 211.

Roderick A. F. MacKenzie, *Introduction to the New Testament*, New Testament Reading Guide Series (Collegeville, Minn.: Liturgical Press, 1960), p. 20.

John L. McKenzie, *Dictionary of the Bible*, p. 243.

Ardis Whitman, "The Courage to Trust," *Reader's Digest*, December 1968, p. 141.

John Patrick, *The Teahouse of the August Moon*, adapted from a novel by Vern Sneider (New York: G. P. Putnam's, 1952).

Detroit Free Press, May 30, 1957, p. 16.

Kilian J. Healy, *Walking with God* (New York: Farrar, Straus & Giroux, 1948), p. 45.

Pliny, *Letters to Trajan*, trans. Mark Link.

John L. McKenzie, *Dictionary of the Bible*, p. 667.

Orley M. Berg, "Seven Reasons for Studying the Book of Revelation," *Ministry* Magazine, January 1978, p. 7.

H. V. Morton, *In the Steps of St. Paul*, pp. 378-79.

Jean-Louis D'Aragon, "The Apocalypse," in *The Jerome Biblical Commentary*, ed. Raymond E. Brown et al. (Englewood Cliffs, N.J.: Prentice-Hall, 1968), p. 475.

Alexander Jones, gen. ed., *The Jerusalem Bible* (New York: Doubleday & Co., 1966), p. 437.

INDEX

Persons

INDEX OF BIBLICAL CITATIONS AND PASSAGES

ACKNOWLEDGMENTS *Continued from page 2*

Excerpts from *Searching the Scriptures* by John J. Dougherty. Copyright 1959 by Doubleday & Co., Inc. Reprinted by permission of Doubleday & Co., Inc.

Excerpts from *The Acts of the Apostles* by Neal M. Flanagan, New Testament Reading Guide Series. Published by The Liturgical Press. Copyrighted by The Order of St. Benedict, Inc., Collegeville, Minnesota.

Excerpt from "A Masque of Reason" from *The Poetry of Robert Frost* edited by Edward Connery Lathem. Copyright 1945 by Robert Frost. Copyright © 1969 by Holt, Rinehart and Winston. Copyright © 1973 by Lesley Frost Ballantine. Reprinted by permission of Holt, Rinehart and Winston, Publishers, Jonathan Cape Ltd., and the Estate of Robert Frost.

Excerpt from "Christian Commune in Evanston" by Michael Hirsley, *Chicago Tribune*, March 5, 1978. Copyrighted, Chicago Tribune. Used with permission.

Excerpts from *To Rule the Night* by James B. Irwin with W. A. Emerson, Jr. (Nashville: Holman Bible Publishers),

pp. 17–18, 22. All rights reserved. Used by permission.

Excerpts from *What Are They Saying About Luke and Acts?* by Robert J. Karras. Copyright © 1979. Reprinted by permission of Paulist Press.

Excerpts from *Dictionary of the Bible* by John L. McKenzie. Copyright © Macmillan Publishing Co., Inc. 1965. Reprinted with permission.

Excerpt from *The Snow Leopard* by Peter Matthiessen. Copyright © 1978 by Peter Matthiessen. Reprinted by permission of Viking Penguin Inc., the author, and Chatto and Windus Ltd., London.

Excerpt from "The Bible, the People's Book" by Carlos Mesters, *Maryknoll Magazine*, June 1981. Reprinted with permission.

Excerpts from *In the Steps of St. Paul* by H. V. Morton. Copyright 1936 by Dodd, Mead & Company, Inc. Copyright renewed 1964 by H. V. Morton. Reprinted by permission of Dodd, Mead & Company, Inc.

"Prayer on a Pencil" by Max Pauli, reprinted from *Prayers for the Time*

Being, copyright © 1971, Liguori Publications, One Liguori Drive, Liguori, Missouri 63057. Used by permission.

Excerpts from *The Journeys of St. Paul* by Stewart Perowne. Copyright © 1973. Reproduced by permission of The Hamlyn Publishing Group Limited, Feltham, Middlesex, England.

Excerpts from *The Life of Paul* by Benjamin Willard Robinson. Copyright 1918 by The University of Chicago. All rights reserved. Published October 1918. Second Edition February 1928. Fourteenth Impression 1949. Reprinted by permission of The University of Chicago Press.

Excerpt from *The Letters of Paul* by Calvin J. Roetzel. Copyright © 1975. Used by permission of John Knox Press.

Excerpt from a personal communication by Robert Rybicki. Reprinted by permission.

Excerpt from *Biblical Archaeology* (Revised and Expanded Edition) by G. Ernest Wright. © 1962 by George Ernest Wright. Used by permission of The Westminster Press and Gerald Duckworth & Co. Ltd., London.

PHOTO CREDITS

214

ABOUT THE AUTHOR

Mark Link has had a remarkable career. He served three years with the Army Air Force in the South Pacific during World War II. Four years later, he graduated as an architect from the University of Cincinnati. Next, he entered the Jesuits and was ordained a priest in 1960. Since then, he has taught at the high school, university, and seminary levels, has written or edited more than 20 books, and has lectured in the U.S. and abroad. Mark Link's last six books include three on Scripture—*These Stones Will Shout* (Old Testament), *The Seventh Trumpet* (Gospels), *Lord, Who Are You?* (Acts, Letters, Revelation)—and three on prayer—*The Mustard Seed* (prayer guide to Mark's Gospel), *You* (beginner's guide to prayer), *Breakaway* (a four-part prayer program for individuals or groups).